Arab and Jewish Women in Kentucky

ARAB AND JEWISH WOMEN IN KENTUCKY

Stories of Accommodation and Audacity

NORA ROSE MOOSNICK

UNIVERSITY PRESS OF KENTUCKY

Copyright © 2012 by The University Press of Kentucky

Scholarly publisher for the Commonwealth,
serving Bellarmine University, Berea College, Centre College of Kentucky,
Eastern Kentucky University, The Filson Historical Society, Georgetown College,
Kentucky Historical Society, Kentucky State University, Morehead State University,
Murray State University, Northern Kentucky University, Transylvania University,
University of Kentucky, University of Louisville, and Western Kentucky University.
All rights reserved.

Editorial and Sales Offices: The University Press of Kentucky
663 South Limestone Street, Lexington, Kentucky 40508-4008
www.kentuckypress.com

16 15 14 13 12   5 4 3 2 1

Cataloging-in-Publication data is available from the Library of Congress.

ISBN 978-0-8131-3621-9 (hardcover : alk. paper)
ISBN 978-0-8131-3622-6 (pdf)
ISBN 978-0-8131-4049-0 (epub)

This book is printed on acid-free paper meeting the requirements of the American
National Standard for Permanence in Paper for Printed Library Materials.

Manufactured in the United States of America.

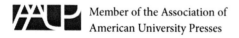 Member of the Association of
American University Presses

Contents

Series Foreword

In the field of oral history, Kentucky is a national leader. Over the past several decades, thousands of its citizens have been interviewed. The Kentucky Remembered series brings into print the most important of those collections, with each volume focusing on a particular subject.

Oral history is, of course, only one type of source material. Yet, by the very personal nature of recollection, hidden aspects of history are often disclosed. Oral sources provide a vital thread in the rich fabric that is Kentucky history.

This volume, the eleventh in the series, weaves together multiple life stories and follows a captivating group of Arab and Jewish women through a narrative journey exploring tradition, assimilation, and Kentucky's cultural landscape. Nora Moosnick's book offers readers a glimpse into the personal lives of these women and provides powerful insights into gender roles and both personal and cultural identity.

The immigrant's story is reemerging in Kentucky's contemporary historical record, and *Arab and Jewish Women in Kentucky: Stories of Accommodation and Audacity* powerfully demonstrates the effectiveness of oral history in documenting that story.

Douglas A. Boyd
James C. Klotter
Terry L. Birdwhistell

PREFACE

I CAME TO THIS PROJECT to honor two men I loved: my father, Monroe Moosnick, and my adopted grandfather, Mousa Ackall. Both men knew fabrics.

My Jewish father's family settled in Versailles, Kentucky, in the hope of making a living from a small dry goods store. My father embraced the store and even aspired to expand it, but his parents had other dreams for their boys—namely, for them to be professionals. Compliance was absolute, so my father became a chemistry professor. Even though he resided in academia, I realize now that his way of being was always that of a merchant. He noticed minor details of other people's clothing and habitually complimented them about the feel or fit of a coat or the make of their shoes. His keen sense of style was reflected in his wardrobe, even though, like a good merchant, he refused to pay the label price for clothes, knowing it was well above the wholesale one. He would wait weeks for the price of a particular item to be slashed before purchasing it.

I accompanied my father on countless weekend jaunts as he (we) shopped for clothes, antiques, or fabrics. It was more than consumer abandon that drove him. It was a serious preoccupation and, perhaps most importantly, it was a social endeavor. Everywhere we went, he knew people, and I thought my father was immensely popular. I was proud that he could barely walk down a street or a mall corridor without being greeted. But when I look back with a sharper eye, I also realize that he was connecting with his own—with Jewish merchants. I remember store owners mumbling to Dad about the current business climate or asking his opinions about such things as the carpets they had chosen for their stores.

There were also non-Jewish merchants, such as Alma at Alma's

Monroe Moosnick. (Author's collection.)

Fabric and Variety Store. It was an adventure (and remains so) to enter her crowded store in what was then the mostly deserted downtown area of Lexington, Kentucky. Hers was a store without aesthetic adornments; customers had to rummage for the material they desired. It was also packed full of colorful characters. I can still see Dad giggling about Alma feeding hot dogs to her crew of small canine companions, whose stomachs tended not to tolerate their "dog food." Her brother sat in his wheelchair at the store, passing the day. Alma talked to Dad like he was another merchant. She'd mumble about the quality of particular fabrics and the effort it took to work with various fabric distributors. She'd gossip with him about "society" customers, and she'd always tell me, "Your father knows this store better than I do." Indeed, he knew exactly where to find a particular fabric, even though it might be covered by several others, because he was always reupholstering something at our home or at the university where he worked. As Alma liked to say, "He knows fabric better than anyone I know."

Over the four decades or so that my father taught at Transylvania University, he befriended numerous students. I am perhaps most boastful of the relationship he built with one Palestinian family, the Ackalls. I can only speculate, but our families might have been drawn to each other out of an appreciation of our likenesses and an understanding of the odd position we held as Jews and Arabs in Kentucky. Multiple generations of Ackalls passed through Transylvania, and our families melded, forming a long and lasting friendship. The eldest member of the family, Mousa—or, as everyone affectionately called him, Sido ("grandfather" in Arabic)—became a grandfather of sorts to me, since mine had died long before I was born.

I spent countless afternoons with Sido, sipping tea in his roomy apartment located close to the University of Kentucky campus (he refused to move to the suburban home his daughter Mary had purchased for him). He shared wonderful stories with me about the fruit trees in Ramallah, the multiple journeys he had made between Palestine and Kentucky, and his encounter with Lawrence of Arabia. He also talked about his days peddling fine linens and rugs throughout the American South. He loved to tell tales of being served tea in southern mansions as he dazzled his customers with his mischievous smile and his ability to speak German,

Mousa Ackall and Nora Moosnick. (Author's collection.)

English, and Arabic. On some afternoons he would open his chest filled with high-end linens, evoking another era. He'd have me feel the quality of the wares and admire the delicate handwork that graced the pieces. I still treasure the hand towels he gave me. Other days we ventured into the closet that housed his numerous expertly stored rugs. He would take them out one at a time, show me the work involved, and explain the country of origin and how he came to own these exquisite pieces. After his death, his family gave me one of his rugs to acknowledge our relationship. My desk chair rests on it as I write these words.

As might be apparent, I am nostalgic about both my father and Sido, who passed long ago. Several years back I decided to honor them by chronicling the stories of other Arab and Jewish merchant families in Kentucky. I believe, as a sociologist, that beyond our individual stories, Kentucky harbors a larger story about immigrants settling in places not traditionally associated with them. Strangely enough, it may be in places such as Kentucky that Arabs and Jews are able to see their likenesses.

Midstream in this work, I decided that women's stories in particular offered an appreciation of Arabs' and Jews' diverse lives in Kentucky and the overlap between them. I took instruction from the people I interviewed and followed my own inclination to enlarge lives that had been doubly overlooked—Arabs and Jews, and women. The stories I heard often involved women playing significant if not dominant roles in the family business. I also realized that focusing on women continued to pay tribute to my father. He reminisced regularly about his mother (more so than about his father), who died weeks after my birth and for whom I am named and to whom I bear an uncanny resemblance. I was told that she sewed at home and for the dry goods store, that she tended to her family as well as to the wider community, and, simply, that she was bold. I have discovered that my grandmother was not alone. There were many women like her, and in this work I give them the credit they are due.

It is certainly the case that men were usually responsible for the situations in which these women found themselves. My New Yorker grandmother would never have chosen to live in Versailles, Kentucky. She followed the entrepreneurial judgment of her Lithuanian husband. In this, her circumstances were representative of those of many women. Yet these women were central figures in their families and in their family businesses. The women whose stories are chronicled in the pages that follow cannot be considered typical Kentuckians. Contrary to contemporary images that reward modern women for breaking free of the home, and unlike Rosie the Riveter, who worked while the men were away, immigrant women have long juggled family and work, as well as the added demands of living in a place that is not their native home. In their stories, common themes emerge between and among Arab and Jewish women having to do with identity, anti-Semitism, success, and gender, among other things.

Through the process of doing this work, I learned more about past generations of women in my family and in my community. I now appreciate that part of my own sense of being different stems from some deep psychological seed planted by my mother. She grew up surrounded by other Jews in Chicago, and she never really felt like a Kentuckian, even though she lived here for more than four decades. I have also gained a new appreciation for Mary, Sido's daughter and a dear friend, who grew

Mary Khayat, Mousa Ackall's daughter. (Photo by Sarah Jane Sanders.)

up in Lexington in the 1940s and 1950s. She was an Arab girl locked out of American customs, including school dances, which Sido found inappropriate. She was, and continues to be, of Palestine, Israel, and Kentucky; her life has always involved physically and metaphysically negotiating these places and their separate ways. She is a Kentuckian and a Palestinian living in Israel, but she is also of the Middle East when she returns to Kentucky.

I have delved into stories that are part of and close to my own. I have also unearthed family history I didn't know existed. My parents and grandparents were not Holocaust survivors, but the social and psychological effects of that horror shook my family. As a child I felt a kind of Jewish badge of honor in being able to claim that I hadn't been affected: "Oh no, we didn't have anyone in the Holocaust." I proudly asserted distance from the whole ordeal. But if I am truly honest and unpeel the coverings, family members I never knew, from another time and place, were nonetheless purged from the earth. As I came to find out, it was mostly the women in my family who were left behind in Lithuania; the males, including my grandfather, had been sent away years earlier to distant lands to avoid conscription into the Russian army. I didn't learn any of this, or about my great-aunts and great-grandparents and their unfortunate fate, until I was in my forties. At that time, after my own parents had passed away, my uncle inquired whether I had found among their things a black metal box filled with letters, written in Yiddish, that my grandfather had sent to his Lithuanian family during World War II. The letters had been returned, stamped "addressee unknown." I never found the letters, even though, in my mind, I can see the box clearly. The letters were always there, in my childhood home, and somehow their spirit infiltrated my psyche. Even though I lived with the false belief that the Holocaust had never directly invaded my family's intimate spaces, it did. Fear was a regular part of our daily lives—a fear so deep that it was not just mine; it came from family members I never knew, yet who spoke to me. What do I do with that fear now, after several generations of my family have led good and comfortable lives in Kentucky? I see other Jews of my generation (I'm forty-seven) and younger who, at least outwardly, do not feel that fear. Maybe my fearful temperament belongs to another, older generation of Jews.

In this work, personal stories are used to explore the depths of experience in an effort to build empathy and insight among and between Arabs and Jews. I use the fearful echoes of previous generations to reach out to Arabs. I think fear is something that Jews and Arabs share. Sometimes fear lies in wait for both of us. Neither Arabs nor Jews can be sure of their footing. Christian and Muslim Arabs (the latter often being comparatively recent immigrants to the United States) may resist fully imparting their stories out of fear that their accounts will be used to further distort and misrepresent them, because they are vulnerable. Their fear is alive, on the surface, and very real. For Jews, fear may be a cultural memory that periodically resurfaces. A dear friend cringed as she listened to a public school administrator introduce a school unit on Hanukkah by referring to the "Jewish race." For my friend, the daughter of a Holocaust survivor, characterizing Jews as a race was too reminiscent of Nazi propaganda. Fear can unite Arabs and Jews. An awareness of vulnerability makes people intensely observant and, potentially, enormously empathetic.

As might be painfully obvious, this work is truly a labor of love. The personal and professional are intricately tied. I am moved by the personal stories that resemble my own. I also engage my sociological eye to see that Arabs and Jews in Kentucky share much in common. Fundamentally, the intention of this book is to reveal, by means of women's tales, their overlapping lives.

During my childhood, I spent countless hours rummaging through the attic, finding items tossed aside years earlier, such as my mother's love letters to my father, which she quickly grabbed from my hands. I would take forgotten photographs and wrap them up as birthday or Mother's Day gifts. In this work, in some sense, I am going through an attic. I hope you find gifts, as I have, in what I have uncovered.

ACKNOWLEDGMENTS

This book did not develop in a vacuum. I had support and a good deal of it. To start, I must thank the men and women who took the time to chat with me, holding enough trust to believe that I would portray their lives with sensitivity.

There are the people who were interviewed, and those who led me to them. All roads lead to Dr. Nadia Rasheed. I know that this project never would have been possible without her unquestioning support.

Others offered sustenance and poignant counsel over the years of pursuing and writing this work. Chief among them are Leslie Guttman, Kate Black, and Rosalind Harris, all of whom hold a wealth of knowledge when it comes to writing and researching and provided sage advice at moments when it was needed. Janet Eldred, early on, discerned those things that were working and those that were not. Marcie Cohen Ferris offered resounding support and useful ideas for making the book better.

Dr. Nadia Rasheed. (Photo by Sarah Jane Sanders.)

Steve Wrinn and the crew at the University Press of Kentucky, including David Cobb and Allison Webster (and not to forget the copyeditor, Linda Lotz), made the publishing process easy, uncomplicated, and straightforward. The quality of the folks at the press is impressive and is a reflection of Steve's creative energy.

Who would have thought that an interaction at a bakery would lead to a sweet and productive friendship? But it did. I often saw Sarah Jane Sanders when I stopped by the bakery where she worked. Serendipitously, she told me that her real passion was photography and directed me to her website: www.sanolaphotography.com. I was overwhelmed by the quality of her work, and soon we were packing up her gear to photograph the people I interviewed. In Sarah I found a friend and fellow documentarian with an intuitive take on this work that, at times, escaped me. It is often said that photographers have a good eye. No doubt, Sarah has one, but the power of her work rests in her ability to couple a good eye with compassion when detecting the essence of people or things.

My family and friends imbue this work—those who have passed away and those who are with me today. I started this project while closing my family home and saying goodbye to childhood memories, to my parents, Monroe and Sonia Moosnick, and to my brother, Les. I ended it bidding farewell to the last of my elders, Marilyn and Franklin Moosnick. While I mourn their passing, I know that I am lucky to have had family members who were so vibrant and engaged in the community.

Lisa and Howard Myers, Madelaine Enochs-Epley, Beth Ellen Rosenbaum, and Liz and Neal Armstrong allowed me the safety of their company when it was a welcome distraction from the book process. Miriam Moosnick never wavered, offering cogent insight daily. I do not know myself beyond her. It is not an exaggeration to say that this project would never have been possible if not for Ted Schatzki. He provided both general support in anticipating the ebbs and flows of writing a book and specific aid as he painstakingly read and reread passages. He is my core, and this work benefitted from his solid dedication to his family. In Louis and Helena Schatzki I see the past, since characters who have passed away long ago surface in them. They also embody the present and future, and they never cease to amaze.

INTRODUCTION

STRONG IMAGES COME TO MIND when thinking about Arabs and Jews and their religions, ethnicities, and lands. Arabs, in particular, are in the public eye and under scrutiny in contemporary America. They are widely viewed as "foreign" and Muslim, an attitude that neglects the many Arabs who may be Christian or secular and those who are not foreign at all but whose families have been American for generations. Treating all Arab Americans as the same deletes not just the larger historical framework of repeated waves of Arab immigrants to America but their individual stories as well.[1] A similar homogenization might apply to Jews, insofar as Americans understand them in relation to the Holocaust or to Israel. It is harder, however, to identify general cultural responses to Jews because, to a great extent, they have simply become Americans whose immigrant roots are, by and large, in the past; Russian Jews are the exception. Jews may also be viewed as the palatable counterpart to Muslim Arabs in the United States, a sentiment that can result in a mix of security and insecurity among Jews, since public sentiment is known to be fickle. Irrespective of how Jews and Arabs are viewed separately, they are inevitably construed as opposing forces engaged in a conflict of biblical and global proportions. Dichotomous renderings of Arabs and Jews overlook the many close and complicated relationships they have forged, both currently and historically. They also ignore the fact that a person can be both Jewish and Arab.

Kentucky is not normally a place that comes to mind when talking about Arabs and Jews. It's not New York or Michigan, where Jews and Arabs abound. "There are Arabs and Jews in Kentucky?" is something I hear regularly—part statement, part question—when I mention my work to people inside or outside the state. Kentucky and Kentuckians are mostly invisible in the United States—that is, they are of no particular interest. When Kentucky does garner outside attention, it is generally portrayed as a poor place whose population is depleted (unless, of course, one is speaking of horses or fried chicken). The common perception is that education and culture flourish elsewhere, but not in Kentucky. I often find myself in the uncomfortable position of defending Kentucky and my continued residence there. Just the other evening, I was told by a visiting academic that I needed to "expand my horizons" because I still live in my hometown. He did not say the same thing to the man sitting next to me who was born and raised in Cape Town, South Africa, and still resides there. It's strange being a Kentuckian among certain learned crowds. An ethos abounds that one can redeem or supersede a Kentucky pedigree by having been educated outside of the state, spending years away, or accomplishing some remarkable feat that overshadows one's Kentucky lineage.

Local interactions, like the one noted above, come as no surprise, given the widespread perceptions that dismiss Kentucky and other states in Appalachia as lacking in diversity and hence sophistication. No doubt, relative to other states, Kentucky's population is not diverse. According to the 2010 census, 7.8 percent of Kentucky's population is black, compared with the 12.6 percent national average. Jews constitute 0.3 percent of Kentucky's population, whereas Jews make up 8.3 percent of New York's population, which translates into more than a million people.[2] Arabs who call Kentucky home constitute less than 1 percent of the state's population. According to 2000 census data, Kentucky's Arab population is 0.18 percent of the total; in Louisville, the state's largest city, Arabs account for 0.47 percent of the population.[3] But statistics do not tell the whole story; instead, they provide demographic snapshots revealing, in this case, that Kentucky's Arab American population is growing. According to the Arab American Institute, "The population who identified as having Arabic-speaking ancestry in the U.S. Census grew by more than 33% between 2000 and 2010. The number of Kentuckians who claim an Arab ancestry more than doubled since the Census first measured ethnic origins in 1980 and is among the fastest growing Arab populations in the country."[4] Numerical summaries offer valuable insights into demographic trends, but they overlook the firsthand accounts of the people living and thriving in Kentucky (and other unlikely locales) who are absent from the popular imagination.

This book challenges misconceptions and seeks to remedy the neglect of Arabs and Jews in out-of-the-way places in America by telling the stories of ten Arab and Jewish women in Kentucky. I aim to confound simplistic notions of Kentucky that offend and belittle. Sundry life experiences unfold in Kentucky. No doubt, some of my Kentucky pride invigorates this work in the hope of disrupting flat portrayals of the state, but there is more to it. I do not wish to do the opposite—that is, to be an advertisement for my home. Instead, I offer a view into lives that are neither one-dimensional nor uniform. I myself have had to negotiate an identity that is both of Kentucky and not of Kentucky. My mother used to say that I was like her—more like a northeasterner than a Kentuckian. Yet I know that my need to please others adheres to my father's Kentucky ways. I cling to a Kentucky identity because it is part of me, but also, to a certain degree, because others disparage it. Similarly, a Muslim woman told me that although she is nonreligious, she publicly owns a Muslim identity because her heritage troubles others.

Equally significant to this book is the showcasing of women's lives. Women's stories may be overwhelmingly consequential in families and in family histories, but they habitually lose currency in larger narratives. This work takes the opposite stance: that women's stories speak to larger themes. In the details of their lives, perceptible overlaps between Arab and Jewish women become apparent. They tell similar tales with common themes: public service to their communities; mother-daughter relations; the agility required to work, mother, and be an active community member; and what it meant to be an Arab or Jewish mother nearly a century ago. Associations materialize in the women's tales, underscoring that lives evolve relationally between generations—mothers and daughters, mothers and sons, aunts and nephews, grandmothers and granddaughters—and within and between communities. Stories may be carried on or fade over the generations, and awareness or the lack thereof may take hold, either reinforcing or negating the fact that stories interlock. Just as an individual's story may be construed as belonging to one person alone and not intrinsically wedded to previous or future generations or to wider contexts, narratives about how immigrant groups become American traditionally spotlight one group at a time and do not consider its correspondence to other groups.[5] I seek to lessen the perceived distance between the Arab and the Jew by way of women's tales. Through the lens of women's lives, the relational links between Arabs and Jews, individuals and communities, and generations become apparent.

This book is grounded in oral history, but it is also informed by socio-logical practices and wisdom. In addition to telling stories, the narrative reflects on the contexts of the stories and the process of gathering them. Although this work is academically informed, drawing on the method-ological and analytical tools of qualitative research practices, it is not an academic work devoted to an academic audience. The focus remains on the stories themselves, and the intent is to reach a wide audience embrac-ing academics and nonacademics alike.

The stories are what matters, and these stories are not widely known, even though Arabs and Jews have established themselves and carved out identities in their diasporas. Arab and Jewish immigrants in the late 1800s and early 1900s came to small communities throughout Kentucky.[6] They brought traditions and boasted looks that betrayed their identities, but they tried to fit in by being cautious and by distancing themselves from the stereotypes shrouding Arabs and Jews. In the 1940s, for instance, my Jewish grandmother knocked on the door of some new Jewish neighbors in Versailles, Kentucky, and said, "We have good relations with the *goyim* [Yiddish for non-Jews] here, don't ruin it," and promptly left. While immi-grants like my grandmother negotiated life in small-town Kentucky, they also encountered and continue to encounter a question asked by their urban counterparts: "What are you doing in Kentucky?" They have become strange hybrids of Middle Eastern traditions and southern manners.

Arabs and Jews have been largely discounted as residents of Kentucky and elsewhere in the region, even though, as business owners, they have provided goods and services for residents in large and small communi-ties across the state for several generations. They are the people who run movie theaters and provide clothes, meats, fine furnishings, shoes, and cell phones, among other items, not to mention the countless professional Arabs and Jews serving their communities as doctors, lawyers, teachers, and so forth. They are deeply ingrained in the larger region. In relating their stories, this book follows the tradition established by many fictional as well as nonfictional works that chronicle the experiences of southern (and Appalachian) Jews.[7]

Jewish and Arab women are adept at telling their stories through the written word.[8] Even so, in the popular mind, the typical southern Jewish peddler and merchant is a man, an image that has obscured the existence of Jewish women entrepreneurs in the region. Comparatively little has been written about the southern Arab American, neglecting both genders. In this book, the stories of ten Arab and Jewish women involved in family businesses are told. In some cases, daughters, sons, or nephews tell the tales of female family members who died years ago; in other cases, the women tell their own stories. Jewish and Christian Arab women whose families came to the United States several generations ago are profiled, along with Arab Muslim women who are relatively new to this country. Along the way, unexpected and largely unknown narratives materialize, not unlike those contained in works such as *Hotel Bolivia: The Culture of Memory in a Refuge from Nazism,* which chronicles the relatively little known story of Jews who fled from Austria to Bolivia during World War II.[9] Similar to *Hotel Bolivia,* this book combines personal narratives with wider observations.

Works like this one, which are based on oral histories, present nuanced stories, and in doing so, they contribute to a body of literature and a discourse that confront misconstructions. Basic notions of Kentucky and the wider region can be challenged via the women's tales, as can stereotypes about Arabs and Jews.[10]

Central to this book is the juxtaposition of the stories of Arabs and Jews. In a political environment where tensions are high between the two groups, even in America, attempts to bring them together are essential. Hussein Ibish poignantly examines the effects of the association between Arabs and terrorists, prevalent in Hollywood films and elsewhere: "So insidious are the processes reinforcing the association between Arabs and terrorism that papers such as this one, which attempt to debunk the stereotypes, may ironically have the subtle effect of further solidifying the association between Arab and terrorism. Until we develop an alternative discourse, however, Arab Americans are going to remain in what may well be the self-defeating position I am taking here, of calling attention to the stereotypes by analyzing and objecting to them." Ibish, though devoted to distortions of Arab Americans specifically, insightfully ties anti-Arab sentiment with anti-Jewish anti-Semitism, noting that they are subtly linked negative forces that create and re-create the greedy "other" with foreign religious practices. "The rise of anti-Arab stereotypes in the United States in recent decades in many ways represents the continued thriving of traditional Western anti-Semitism, in a new guise. The caricature of Semitic racial characteristics that typifies traditional Western anti-Jewish imagery has been largely transferred to the Arab as overt anti-Jewish anti-Semitism has fallen out of fashion. The similarities between the image of the wealthy, filthy, greedy, vulgar oil sheikh and anti-Jewish imagery are obvious."[11]

Ibish draws anti-Semitic parallels between men, but historically, both Arab and Jewish women have been misunderstood as overbearing hypernurturers, docile and silent sufferers, or sexually exotic beings.[12] Placing these women side by side shows that such broad and sweeping characterizations disregard the intricacies of their lives. For instance, the Myers sisters of Hopkinsville, Kentucky, never married or had children, but from the 1930s to the 1980s they were movers and shakers in their community and in their elegant women's dress shop. These unlikely Jewish Kentuckians longed for New York, however. "Don't bury me in Hopkinsville," they repeatedly implored their only nephew. Or consider the life of Teresa Isaac. This contemporary Arab American politician was the mayor of Lexington, the second largest city in Kentucky, from 2002 to 2006. In some ways, she is like any other politician, raising funds and shaking the hands of countless people. Unlike other politicians, however, she claims an Arab American identity. And unlike other Arab American Christians with long roots in this country, she does not shun Muslim Arabs; instead, she reaches out to them publicly. She also acknowledges her roots in the Appalachian Mountains of Kentucky. "I identify very much with the mountains, very much with the mountains, and always when I meet somebody else from the mountains, it's like there is an automatic connection. Somebody tells me they're from around Harlan, and it feels like an immediate connection, even if I have never met them before. I feel like an immediate bond, the same way I would feel if somebody came up and said that they were Lebanese; it's the same feeling if they tell me they are from the mountains." In the women's stories, insights appear, revealing individual as well as common experiences of being an Arab or Jew in Kentucky.

Intersection between the experiences of Arabs and Jews is carved into the structure of the book. In each of the four chapters in which stories are related (chapters 2–5), the narratives of Jewish women and Arab women are paired around a common theme. Sarah and Frances Myers and Teresa Isaac are linked in the chapter titled "Publicly Exceptional" because they are women who excelled, visibly and dramatically, in their Kentucky communities and beyond. The stories of Elsie Nasief and Gishie Bloomfield are joined in the chapter "Maternal Echoes" because their narratives speak to mother-daughter relations and the mothering expectations associated with Jewish and Arab women. The image of the overstressed modern mother trying to negotiate work, kids, and community obligations is known to most Americans, even if the standard image is not of a Muslim or Jewish Kentuckian. In the chapter "Into Focus," Manar Shalash, Sawsan Salem, and Renee Hymson are introduced to make maternal lives more visible. Manar and Sawsan are contemporary Muslim mothers in Kentucky, openly balancing the multiple demands placed on any mother; in contrast, the maternal juggling act that Jewish Renee performed during the 1950s and 1960s went largely unnoticed by others. All three, however, have had to face larger reactions that underestimated and negated the full reality of their lives. Finally, Rose Rowady and Rose Moosnick, profiled in the chapter titled "Archetypal and Distant Figures," represent the many immigrant and transplanted women whose primary focus was the success of their children—their ability to overcome financial and social struggles and enter the professional classes, with all the comforts that accompany upward mobility.

Many other stories are embedded in those of the ten women told here. I gathered a cacophony of both Arab and Jewish voices, even though only a selection of them is featured in this book. Additional voices are woven into the main stories by way of direct quotes and references. Beyond the stories captured in the confines of formal interviews, there are also observations drawn from everyday interactions with friends and others, both Jewish and Arab. Despite the diversity of the stories, this work is narrow; it is a far cry from being exhaustive or universal in its reach. There are many other related stories in Kentucky and elsewhere, ranging from those of female entrepreneurs to the experiences of non-Arab and non-Jewish women who marry into Arab and Jewish families.

The ten accounts related in this book are surrounded by other narratives having to do with the context behind the highlighted stories. A prime example of contextualizing, explored in chapter 1, is the sensitive, slippery, and untidy nature of identity. Eighty-something Elsie Nasief loves University of Kentucky basketball and is proud of her devotion to the program, but she's equally proud of her trips to Lebanon to visit family. She is of Kentucky while also connecting with family elsewhere. Rose Moosnick, my grandmother, knew full well that she and her family were inherently different from the other inhabitants of Versailles, Kentucky, in the 1920s and 1930s. Her son, Franklin Moosnick, put it plainly: "You couldn't *not* understand that you were different from, that you were unique in a town of 1,100 people. You knew that you were one out of 1,100, and that they had an innate sense that there was something not right with you, and that you were tainted in some way." Other intricacies include the delicate dance that many Arabs and Jews perform while simultaneously negotiating Kentucky and the Middle East and the diversity of businesses and work relationships they maintain.

The postscript, "On Being a Documentarian," further contextualizes the women's stories by briefly touching on some of the challenges and uncertainties associated with oral history and the related enterprises that document individuals' lives. I ask how, in this age of celebrity culture, recorders of stories can capture authentic accounts. Other questions include whether documentarians necessarily perpetuate the contemporary Western cultural belief, overtly nourished by reality television, that telling one's story holds out the prospect of fame. Might the documentarian be the one seeking notoriety, rather than the person who opens up his or her life? Finally, how do documentarians maneuver in a larger cultural landscape that erases the historical contexts of events?

Contextualizing also includes the concept of marginalization. It's not a stretch to associate Arabs and Jews with marginalization, particularly Arab American Muslims. Nadine Naber argues that Arab Americans traverse a racially charged landscape that may offer them the advantages of whiteness, but since 9/11, they are more often marginalized and racialized, an experience common to earlier immigrant groups. Naber explains, "I use the term anti-Arab racism to locate Arab Americans' marginalization within the context of U.S. histories of immigrant exclusion (e.g., the history of Asian exclusion, anti-Mexican racism, and Japanese internment) in which the racialization of particular immigrants as different than and inferior to whites has relied upon culturalist and nationalist logics that assume that 'they' are intrinsically unassimilable and threatening to national security."[13] Not surprisingly, according to Naber, Arab Americans are hypervisible but far from understood. In a cultural environment that misconstrues Muslim Arab Americans in particular, these individuals know the power and currency of their words: what they say can either boost understanding or be used to further misrepresent them.

Business owners, because they move in the public realm, are particularly aware of this dilemma, irrespective of their racial or ethnic background. They know that public pronouncements or actions can harm their livelihoods. To illustrate, Teresa Isaac recalls that one of her uncles consciously decided to remove himself from the Lebanese American community to boost his business. "My uncle used to always say, 'I'm not Arab American. I'm American.' We'd invite him to the *Haflis* [Lebanese social gatherings] and all that, and he wouldn't want to go. He wouldn't want to have anything to do with it, but he also felt like he would lose business if people knew. He wanted to be American, not an Arab American. He thought people wouldn't do business with him." Private businesses can also be sites of political action. Sarah and Frances Myers crossed racial boundaries in Hopkinsville, Kentucky, in the 1950s when they were the first to allow their African American employees to operate the cash register. According to their nephew, Howard Myers, "In most of the stores in Hopkinsville, even if they did have African American employees, somebody else would handle the money, but they [Sarah and Frances] were determined. When I say they were determined, that was from the fifties, before all that [the civil rights movement] happened in the sixties."

Framing the stories in this book with marginalization in mind is not easy, however, due to the fact that marginalization applies to some of the Arabs and Jews in Kentucky some of the time, but not to all of them all of the time. Some of the interviewees would not choose marginalization as a theme for narrating their lives or the lives of their families. For many, life has been good in Kentucky, and it is success that defines them. Marginalization, therefore, is a sticky concept because an individual's or group's social location is in constant flux. Additionally, individual interpretations vary. In my estimation, "real" stories—tales that impart lives in all their contours—must acknowledge the strange position of the Arab and Jew in Kentucky: sometimes privileged, sometimes neutral, and sometimes marginalized. The challenge confronting a work that aspires to reach non-academic communities and to take instruction from the interviews themselves is to negotiate multiple conversations and, at times, the disjuncture between the words shared and the academic discourse that partly infuses this work. Ultimately, I use marginalization as a site of union between Arabs and Jews.

The dividing line that designates some individuals or groups as familiar, safe, or native and others as alien, foreign, or nonnative can become blurred and obscured in the larger culture, as well as in the intimate settings of communities, families, and individuals. Social boundaries alter with intermarriage and can vary within families and over generations, since one family member may look more "Jewish" or "Arab" than another.

Identities can be everywhere and nowhere. Being the "other" is not uniformly experienced. And some of the interviewees directed attention away from what might be considered tales of marginalization. In works based on oral traditions, interviewees may not see themselves as marginalized (and they may not be so), or they may treat marginalization as a thing of the past. Maternal accounts, for instance, can resonate with a son even if the marginalization embedded in the maternal anecdote is not stressed. One interviewee shared a story his mother had told him about the time her Jewish father needed to get to his business in western Kentucky during a Ku Klux Klan rally: "My mother used to tell the story about my grandfather having to go to the plant one night, and he knew the Klan was going to circle, so he put his white sheet on and went on down and checked things out." Although the use of a disguise clearly documents his grandfather's sensitivity to marginalization, the narrator told the story to highlight not his grandfather's marginalization but his ingenuity. It appears that this was a story the mother wanted her son to know, but her intention in passing it on is not clear.

The preceding account attests to the strange topography Jews (and, I would add, Arab Americans) must traverse. Marginalization among American Jews and Arabs (particularly Christian Arab Americans) may be something of the past or something fleeting, coming in and out of focus based on people's appearances. It may be further complicated when Arabs and Jews enjoy financial success. Some groups may experience unconditional marginalization, but the situations are never homogeneous. Take Muslim women, for instance. Sawsan Salem and Manar Shalash point out that women who wear the *hijab* experience a sense of difference that is avoided by Muslim women who do not cover their heads. Sawsan and Manar, as well as other Muslim women I have come to know in Kentucky, tell me they lead happy and contented lives. The question I am struggling with is this: what makes Jews and Arab Americans different or marginalized when they live comfortable or privileged lives and their stories are marked by success and acclimation?

I now return to the notion of fear introduced in the preface. Arabs and Jews are often acutely aware that public sentiment is unstable, and they may share a fear that their situations are not secure (or may not remain so). One has to look no further than the controversy over building a mosque in Lower Manhattan, near the former site of the World Trade Center, to appreciate the volatility of public sentiment. Likewise, after shots were fired near a mosque outside of Nashville, a representative said point-blank that members of her community "feared" breaking the fast together as they normally did during Ramadan. One might ask whether, for Jews, fear is a thing of the past. But consider Bernie Madoff. His infamous misdeeds reverberated in the Jewish community not only because of the money he siphoned from his own people but also, and perhaps more insidiously, because of how he publicly represented Jews: he fit all the negative stereotypes. The question is whether Madoff's offenses will usher in a surge of anti-Semitism. I have also seen a hint of fear among Christian Arab Americans. A Palestinian Christian woman makes a point of wearing a cross to publicly confront the misperception that being Arab and being Muslim are one and the same. Another Palestinian interviewee stays clear of politics: "I [do] not join any organization or club or anything like that. You are in politics. I'm completely out. Me and my family leave the politics for somebody else." The interviewees of Lebanese descent expressed the least degree of fear, although it sometimes surfaced, as in the case of Teresa Isaac's uncle. In contrast, Teresa overwhelmingly emphasizes her own fearlessness.

The focus on fear and marginalization that I associate with Arabs and Jews, regardless of their religious background, is mainly mine. I am attentive to such matters because I am a sociologist. How, then, should I manage the words shared with me? It is important to note that managing other people's words requires constant negotiation and a revelation of the context, including the orientation the documentarian brings to the work. I still recall Katherine Borland's powerful work "That's Not What I Said: Interpretive Conflict in Oral Narrative Research," in which she asks, "How might we present our work in a way that grants the speaking women interpretive respect without relinquishing our responsibility to provide our own interpretation of her experience?" Borland had interviewed her grandmother and, based on her stories, labeled her a feminist, only to face her grandmother's protestations that she was not a feminist and her insistence that the feminist branding be withdrawn. That left Borland to ponder, "Who controls the text?"[14] Any work that documents lives, I would argue, faces similar concerns.[15] Let me illustrate from this work.

Earlier, I repeated an anecdote about my grandmother, whom I never met. The story of my grandmother confronting some new neighbors, as told here, resonates with my impression of both my family and my grandmother. The familial message my parents relayed to me during childhood was that we were to be polished Jews and thus avoid the stereotypes shrouding New York Jews. It also jibes with my impression of my grandmother as a forceful woman. The version of the story I repeated here had been told to me by the former neighbors themselves—the objects of her admonition. But when I asked my uncle for his input, he altered the story to read as follows: "Rose knocked on the new neighbors' door after the new residents had a run-in with a neighbor and said only, 'We have good relations with the *goyim* here. Don't ruin it.' She left without another word." He changed the story only slightly, but it is decidedly different. The neighbors claimed that they had just arrived in Versailles, but my uncle's version gives the impression that they had been in town long enough to offend some of the locals. It makes my grandmother look much less forceful and her actions look more appropriate, since the neighbors had already quarreled with others. Which is the accurate story? I don't know. I must, however, acknowledge my desire to promote my own interpretation of my grandmother, as well as my uncle's possible interest in portraying his mother more gently and positively.

There are additional contexts surrounding this book. Arabs and Jews (and their stories) are often presented as existing side by side in the Middle East but not in communities across the United States, even though Middle Eastern conflicts have a political life in this country. Weaving together stories in the United States, moreover, highlights immigrants' evolution into Americans, as well as the interlocking relationships among ethnic groups. Long ago, my aunt from New York sat at my family's Passover table in Lexington and complained, "The only thing wrong with London is that there are too many Arabs." My aunt could seemingly distinguish Arabs and Jews on the streets of London but not at the Passover table in Kentucky, because she was sitting next to Sido's daughter Mary, whom my aunt mistook as a Jew. My aunt made an offhand remark when she thought she was securely nestled among Jews. I describe her private words because they offer a window into the lives of immigrants and their descendants and into the sensitive relations among Arabs, Jews, and others.

In my assessment, knocking down misrepresentations of Arabs and Jews necessitates addressing the palpable tension between and among the two groups and those outside their communities. Distrust surfaces even in Kentucky. Relations between faraway Israel and Palestine can make local interactions difficult or even impossible, and Arabs and Jews may perpetuate stereotypes about each other. I've been told by Arab Christians that Jewish women spent time in their family stores because they wanted to watch over the money. Some Christian Arabs with Lebanese roots have told me point-blank that they don't like Muslims because they associate Muslims with Ottoman rule in Lebanon. Some Jews have not been shy about telling me that Arabs are not to be trusted. Young Muslim girls have counseled their mothers to decline my invitation to chat because I am Jewish; the girls conflate Israeli Jews and American ones. I chronicle such chatter not to blame anyone; disparaging remarks are not the property of any one person or group. My interviewees may actually be much less inclined to engage in such talk because they willingly participated in a work devoted to both Arabs and Jews. Nonetheless, both Arabs and Jews stereotype the other, and both groups, of course, are stereotyped by non-Arabs and non-Jews. (One Arab told me, "I'm asked daily, 'What are you?'") I believe honesty is needed to dispel myths and create dialogue.

I aspire to create a conversation between Arabs and Jews through the stories told here in authentic voices. It is in the telling of real stories that sweet ones sometimes appear. Sweet stories are emerging in Kentucky communities: at events where Muslims and Jews jointly participate in the breaking of the fast at Ramadan, and at Middle Eastern restaurants where Jews and Muslims build camaraderie. Sweet stories emanate from more private settings, too. When Rose Marie Farah, a Lebanese American, bade me farewell after we had chatted for several hours during our first meeting, she hugged me good-bye and uttered, "I love you." Possibilities reside in honest, difficult, real, and sweet stories between and among Arabs and Jews in Kentucky.

Essentially, it is my hope that this book will contribute to local and national efforts to create connections between Arabs and Jews in the face of the tensions that bedevil them, even in Kentucky.[16] By way of these women's tales, Arabs and Jews can affirm their likenesses, differences, and humanity, and they can do so in places far removed from both the Middle East and the typical U.S. locales associated with these peoples.

1

COMPLEXITIES

THIS WORK IS MULTILAYERED and polyphonic. The seemingly simple assertion that it is about Arab and Jewish women with businesses in Kentucky proves misleading. This chapter is therefore committed to multiplying the dimensions of the stories told and exposing the many tiers that exist. Characterizing the interviewees as immigrants is inaccurate, because not all of them are; in addition, it neglects the complicated relationship Arabs and Jews have with the Middle East. Identities are also complicated. Identifying oneself as an Arab or a Jew may have to do with religious inclinations, Middle Eastern associations, or identification as such by non-Arabs and non-Jews because of one's outward appearance or name. Voice is also complicated. While I am determined to uncover Arab and Jewish women's tales, it is sometimes the men who do the talking because their mothers, aunts, or grandmothers have passed away and are not here to tell their stories. Discrepancies also emerge in relation to the businesses. For some of the women, their businesses defined their own and their families' identities; for others, the business was just a passing preoccupation. And the variable and dynamic larger business climate influenced the intimate decisions women and their families made about how they earned a living. It is to these topics that I now turn.

IMMIGRANT STATUS

I often describe this book as devoted to immigrants' voices, even though, more often than not, I interviewed not the immigrants themselves but their descendants. Most of the interviewees were first-, second-, or (in a few cases) third-generation Kentuckians; a smaller number of them were immigrants who came to this country within the last fifty years. (Making matters more complicated, some interviewees were second-generation Kentuckians on one side of the family and first-generation Kentuckians on the other side.) Descendants were asked to look back, relying on family tales and memories, to provide a portrait of a grandmother, mother, or aunt. The stories of those who passed away long ago are thus narrated by family members who speak in the present with an eye toward the past.

With the multiple voices narrating as well as embodying the stories, it is not surprising that my use of the term *immigrant* has sometimes been misleading. For instance, when I told an Arab contact that I was interested in interviewing Arab and Jewish immigrant businesswomen, she explained that although her sister had once owned a business in Kentucky, she did not qualify because she had been born in the United States. To her, the term *immigrant* implied place of birth. But I believed that her sister would be a valid subject because her parents had been born in the Middle East, much of the family still identified with the region and were considered atypical Kentuckians, and their lives were marked by movement between the Middle East and Kentucky. The former business owner, however, chose to distance herself from her family's desire to associate with their country of origin. This phenomenon, whereby people select their own identities, is addressed later in this chapter, but a couple of thoughts surfaced from this conversation. Those persons who are closer to being immigrants are aware of the significance of the label and the precision with which it is applied, and they may feel a need to distance themselves from the status of immigrant. In contrast, those who have been in Kentucky for a generation or more do not feel the need to do so; they are often proud to claim their immigrant roots as something quaint or unique, like a cherished native food dish.

Immigration is not the unidirectional model of assimilation that civics books previously led us to believe. The melting pot image, whereby immigrants (or, rather, their children) shed the family's country of origin to become American, does not fully capture the truth. Immigrants are actually multidirectional: they can embrace their homes in the United

States and appreciate their roots in another place simultaneously. This is particularly true for newer immigrants. Sawsan Salem, who immigrated from Jordan nearly two decades ago, characterized her adjustment to the United States: "First, I think I was like a stranger. I did not [get] used to it until a while ago, but now I like it, and love being here. And I love too my country." Televisions and radios playing in the background during interviews, broadcasting news in Arabic or Russian, suggested unbroken ties to the "old country," which, though old, was not relegated to the past. Mothers looked forward to taking summer trips to Palestine or Jordan with their children, using the opportunity to teach the children Arabic and educate them about their culture of origin. Identities were thus both American and other.

The multidirectional nature of their lives is also multigenerational. Grandmothers divide their time between America and Palestine or Jordan. One child aspired to eventually live in Jordan rather than in Kentucky; other children, while visiting overseas, had to temper their American ways that clashed with Middle Eastern customs; and some children simply preferred the United States, even though they understood their lives in relation to elsewhere. Salim Natour (who has passed away since our interviews) had not returned to Palestine since the 1960s. He dreamed about the land he left behind, but at the same time, he understood why he had to leave Palestine and that Ramallah was not a good place for his children. "Sometimes I dream about Ramallah," he said. "I dream about what I saw when I was in Ramallah when I was very young. I [would] like to go visit, but not to live. When I went it was 1965. All my friends from school, they left the country. They have no job. They went to Egypt, Saudi Arabia, Syria, Lebanon. All my friends just left. Over there, too much trouble. You can't make a decent living. Fighting, bombing, killing. That's why I left." Salim's oldest daughter expressed similar sentiments to her father after visiting Palestine: "My oldest daughter, she visit once," he said. "She said, 'Dad, it was nice to visit, not to live,' 'cause over there, so many things happened. You're afraid to go to the market and come back alive. Suicide bombing, it's dangerous." Although Salim had no intention of resettling in Palestine, Ramallah maintained an obvious presence in the family. Salim's wife, Nahil, left our conversation early on a weekday morning to take a call from her sister in Ramallah. Salim and Nahil's son,

Victor, had married a woman from Ramallah, and the young couple had to negotiate getting in and out of Palestine for return visits.[1]

For Jews, the "elsewhere" is often not the family's country of origin. It is not uncommon for Jews to be unsure where their families migrated from. They may know that their ancestors came from somewhere in Poland, Lithuania, or Russia, and they may even know the name of a *shtetl* (a Jewish village). But because of the persecution of the Jews and the disappearance of many of their communities during World War II, physical links to the past are mostly absent. I heard about parents and grandparents from eastern Europe who disassociated themselves from their ancestral land. Simone Salomon remembered her Lithuanian grandmother's lack of emotional attachment to Europe, even though "she was very old country. There were all these things that she couldn't understand, like why people were going to Europe. She said, 'Who would want to go there?' She didn't believe in traveling. She said, 'After you are dead, what difference does it make where you have been?'"

With old-country ties dissolved, attention focused on Israel. Israel often arises in conversations among Jews whose families settled in Kentucky years ago: individuals have taken trips to Israel, family members have settled there, money has been sent, and people care about the country's well-being. Sarah and Frances Myers were part of the community of Hopkinsville, Kentucky, but they were also supportive of Israel. "My aunt Frances wore a little star of David as a charm," reported Howard Myers. "They saw themselves as very assimilated in the community, but it's not like they went around saying, 'I'm Jewish.' They would buy some war bonds from Israel. They were supportive of Israel." The degree of interest in Israel varied among the interviewees. Every Jew I spoke to had either been to Israel or desired to go, but for the most part, their daily lives were divorced from the region.

Among Arab American Christians whose families immigrated years ago from Lebanon, there was little talk about the younger generation returning to Lebanon and not much focus on the Middle East. Only Teresa Isaac talked about her own work in the Middle East and mentioned that her children are interested in the region's politics and current events. This is more consistent with the children of newer Arab immigrants, who are highly aware of the political firestorm surrounding Palestine and Israel.

By and large, children and grandchildren of Lebanese immigrants seem disconnected from their roots.[2] This is not unexpected; as Teresa's uncle, Joe Isaac, explained, "We tried very hard to get information from Lebanon and couldn't get anything. So really our history almost starts on this shore." In America, members of the younger generation connect with their ancestral past largely through food. They have intermarried; their children and grandchildren may be blond, and they may not even identify themselves as Arab Americans. Joe mused, "See, like if my father was living today, he would see one of my grandchildren who is blue-eyed." Unlike the younger generation, their grandparents and great-grandparents who first brought their families to Kentucky never lost sight of being Lebanese. Trips back and forth were not uncommon for some of the first Lebanese immigrants who settled in Kentucky from the early 1900s to the 1920s.[3] Even in later years, during the 1960s and 1970s, movement between Lebanon and Kentucky flourished for some families.

One of them was the family of Rose Marie Farah from Carlisle, Kentucky. Rose Marie's parents had come from Lebanon, and she remained committed to her background. She married someone from Lebanon, traveled to that country, attended Lebanese conventions in the United States, cooked Lebanese food, spoke Arabic, and, perhaps most noteworthy, arranged for her husband's Lebanese family to settle in Kentucky. She was not long married and four months' pregnant when his first family members arrived. "What was I going to do with them?" she asked. "They didn't speak English or anything. And thank God I had a few extra rooms. I wasn't prepared or anything. We got them a head start and I had to translate and take them to the dentist and tell them don't bite your tongue in Arabic. It was five months before we could get them a house of their own." Rose Marie eventually helped relocate numerous family members from Lebanon to small-town Kentucky, and today, "Everybody has done well, and we all get together."

Elsie Nasief gave less attention to the flow of family and friends between Kentucky and Lebanon and more consideration to her own trips to Lebanon to visit family still living there, to see her parents' villages, and, in some sense, to pay homage to her mother. Elsie's mother left Lebanon a couple of years after World War I and thought that she would return someday. "She [Elsie's mother] told me that the last night she was in Lebanon she slept with her mother. And her mother told her, 'I'll never see you again.' My mother said, 'Yeah, we're going there, make money, and come back.' Her mother said, 'You'll never come back.'" Elsie also maintains strong ties with the Orthodox church that her father, along with other Lebanese immigrants in Louisville, cofounded, thereby respecting both her mother's and father's memories. As might be expected, Elsie identified herself as Lebanese American. She called other women and female friends "Lebanese ladies." Certainly, there is some correspondence between the strength of her identity and her attachment to the Middle East, among other factors.

IDENTITY

Notions of identity lurked implicitly and explicitly in the conversations. Identities are wide ranging among Arab and Jewish Kentuckians; these identities can also be singular or multiple and labile. Identities are intricate creatures, and this is especially true for Arabs and Jews in Kentucky, a location that doesn't attract many others like them. But interpretations of their place in that location vary. One interviewee said she "always had an inferiority complex" as an Arab American in Kentucky, whereas others seemed unfazed by their backgrounds. Some are proud to own and to publicly acknowledge being an Arab or a Jew. Others prefer to shed their ancestral past and proudly assert that they no longer carry any markers that would link them to their Arab or Jewish heritage: they are Kentuckians and Americans.

Identities can be tied to how others classify individuals, in both a reinforcing and an oppositional manner. The illusive nature of identity surfaced not just in the interviews but also in the process of locating potential interviewees. A friend suggested a prospective Jewish interviewee to me, describing the woman as "coming from a Jewish family that had a store in a small community in central Kentucky." When I called the woman and told her of my interest in Arab and Jewish families with businesses in Kentucky, she responded that neither she nor her family was Jewish. When I relayed this information to my friend, she quipped, "She doesn't want to admit it, but her father was Jewish." According to a man I'll call "Nicholas," the majority of immigrants from the former Soviet Union who have settled in this country in the past couple of decades are Jewish but prefer to self-identify as Russian. If sought out for interviews, these Jews would be disinclined to talk for fear of being publicly branded as Jewish. Quite the opposite, the individuals depicted in this work self-identified as Jewish or Arab, but they did so in varying degrees and expressed their identities in different ways. I briefly explore this variation to illustrate the difficulties associated with naming and pinpointing identities.

Some interviewees were most decidedly Arab or Jewish but also Kentuckians. Attachment to Kentucky basketball and to Palestine or Lebanon was a common theme. Others uttered sentiments indicating that they could never fully reconcile themselves with Kentucky. "I'm different" was their refrain. Some were not completely comfortable either in Kentucky or in urban settings such as New York. Others carried an awareness of difference even among their own. Sarah and Frances Myers, for instance, were more polished than New York Jews and at times had more in common with non-Jews in their small Kentucky town than with their Jewish counterparts. According to their nephew, "They were much more integrated into the larger community, like being members of the Chamber of Commerce, where my memory is [that] most of the other Jews tended to not be as high profile in those civic, community kind of things."

In the interviews, an assortment of factors were mentioned that strengthened or weakened Arab and Jewish identities in Kentucky. Whether one's mother, aunts, and grandmothers claimed to be Jewish or Arab mattered. Equally vital was where one was raised. Jews and Arabs from the larger communities of Louisville and Lexington talked about the strong, secure Arab or Jewish communities they knew as children in the 1940s, 1950s, and 1960s. Even earlier, in the 1930s, Elsie Nasief grew up surrounded by immigrants in the Haymarket section of Louisville. "Oh, I tell ya, we were around the Jews, the Italians, and Lebanese people that's on Jefferson, and most of the Lebanese people lived in one area." Those who were isolated in rural and small-town Kentucky, meanwhile, grasped what it meant to be different. Recall (from the introduction) that Rose Moosnick's son was fully aware of being different in Versailles, Kentucky, in the 1920s and 1930s. What is curious about Rose's situation, as well as that of the Myers sisters, is that being different in a small community did not preclude them from striving for and achieving public and civic success. In these cases, families did not retreat because they were different; instead, they became public citizens, and it may have been their unique and isolated positions that motivated them to excel.

Physical location, as well as social location, can have a bearing on identity. Equally powerful are outward appearances. Identity may reflect whether one can shed one's ethnic or religious background in public. Can outside observers easily peg an individual as an Arab or a Jew? Do non-Arabs and non-Jews notice when they encounter someone who is presumably nonnative? Today, intermarriage has given rise to an expanding cast of characters—such as Gwyneth Paltrow and Harrison Ford (with Jewish backgrounds) and Vince Vaughn and Kristy McNichol (with Arab backgrounds)—who bear no marks of their ethnic or religious backgrounds. As a result, their self-identity may not be defined at all by their Arab or Jewish descent. The identities of others—such as Paula Abdul and Jerry Seinfeld, who have both Arab and Jewish backgrounds—are confusing.

Locally, Will Crane, whose mother is Jewish and father is not, wrote about his experiences growing up "Half Jewish," as he titled his paper for an independent study project with me. Will said, "The most common response I get when I tell people that I'm Jewish is, 'Really? But you don't look Jewish.' With my twenty-six years of experience of not looking Jewish, I have yet to understand what exactly this means. Is it better to look Jewish than not to look Jewish? In my specific case, I am Jewish but do not fit the stereotype that has been associated with being Jewish. As a result, this has led to different and sometimes unique experiences. The way I look has allowed me to assimilate more easily into non-Jewish society. However, it has also opened the door for anti-Semitic remarks that might not have been said if someone knew I was Jewish."

Will's mother, Janice Crane, found her son's characterization of himself as half Jewish surprising. Identity struggles or the lack thereof can vary between mother and son. "Unlike my son, I do have what some people would call typical Jewish characteristics," said Janice, "including growing up with a last name of Steinberg. I was a little surprised with Will's feelings growing up, as he put it, half Jewish. From my perspective, the way he was raised and according to Jewish law, he's Jewish, not half Jewish. I do understand that his father's side of the family isn't Jewish. They celebrate Christmas, and although they respect and support his being Jewish,

Will and Janice Crane. (Courtesy Crane family.)

they probably don't or can't understand his personal religious struggles. In retrospect, I'm not sure I understood them either. While there were some similarities, our experiences were quite different. I grew up in a kosher home, with the synagogue as the center of my parents' social life. In fact, almost all my parents' friends were Jewish. My sons grew up in a home where there was a greater diversity of friends and family. Someone's religious views were not important factors in our social circle. While the synagogue was important, especially during the years they studied for their bar mitzvahs, it was not central to their lives. I thought his not looking Jewish and having Christian family members would protect him from anti-Semitic sentiments. I wanted him to not see being Jewish as a burden, but as a spiritual path that could give him guidance in how he lived his life. In spite of what he might have felt, something must have worked, because he's grown up to be a wonderful young man with a kind and good heart."

Identity gaps surface between mothers and sons, and confusion over ethnicity can occur, even among one's own. Palestinian Manar Shalash is often misidentified, even by other Arabs. "I get a lot of people think that I'm Hispanic, Mexican," she said. "I got a lady today. She's from Iraq, and she goes, 'You look Italian.' I said, 'I do! I've never had that before. I've heard Mexican, but never, never Italian.' And she was talking to me and I said, 'You don't look like you're from Iraq.' She said, 'Yeah, a lot of people think I'm Hispanic too!'" Racial and ethnic boundaries can bewilder even those within them.

Even when one's "different" looks cannot be discarded, one can attempt to distance oneself from stereotypes. Unlike some of the other Jewish merchants in western Kentucky, when Sarah and Frances Myers went on buying trips to New York in the 1950s through 1970s, they took advantage of the cultural opportunities there rather than visiting only Jewish attractions and institutions. Their nephew remembered, "They were urban. They liked the pace of New York. They liked eating out, but getting back to the Jewish, it was all the assimilated world of New York. Other Jewish families would always go to the delis and that kind of thing when they went to New York. There was this other family that had a business . . . a general merchandising kind of thing—boots, jeans, Boy Scouts stuff, that kind of thing. They would go to New York once or twice a year, but they would go to the theater a little bit, and they would go to the delis, whereas Sarah and Frances were going to the Algonquin and eating at what was the premier—what they perceived as the premier—[restaurant], as opposed to what I perceive as the Jewish part of [the city], and they didn't have any relatives up there either." Others unconditionally owned being Arab or Jewish. Simone Salomon affirmed her identity succinctly: "The first thing I think about myself is that I'm Jewish. Just about everything about [me is] Jewish."

By owning an Arab or Jewish identity, a person can also claim the knowledge base that accompanies it, and knowledge can create boundaries. Sociologist Patricia Hill Collins recognized in her classic work *Black Feminist Thought* that knowledge can develop from being an outsider within. Collins was referring to the depth of insight cultivated by black women working as domestics in the intimate spaces of white homes, even though they were not full members of these families. These women knew both the white world they inhabited during the day and their own black communities, which were hidden from white gazes.[4] Similar thinking can be applied to Arabs and Jews who are both Kentuckians and outsider observers, enjoying perspectives that are not widely known. Let me illustrate through the following example.

One day I was having lunch in Winchester, Kentucky, with two friends, eighty-something Sylvia Green and ninety-something Mike Rowady. Sylvia and Mike are dear longtime friends who feel completely comfortable with each other. Sylvia is a Holocaust survivor, and Mike is of Arab descent. During lunch, a woman in her fifties who was neither Arab nor Jewish conversed with Sylvia and Mike. She said, "Mrs. Green, I was just in Washington and went to the Holocaust Museum. Have you been there?" Mrs. Green responded, "No, honey, I lived it. I don't need to go to the museum." The woman then turned to Mike and asked, "Mr. Rowady, do you remember my father?" "Of course I remember your father," replied Mike. "My mother always recognized his shoes in the Ku Klux Klan parades." The woman good-naturedly admitted that she wasn't surprised about her father. Several notable things stand out from this interaction. Mike's and Sylvia's atypical identities are part of their daily lives and are noted by themselves, by those close to them, and by others. The woman in the restaurant sympathetically acknowledged difference vis-à-vis Mrs. Green, and Mr. Rowady inserted difference of his own accord.

It's not surprising that their identities include difference. Sylvia carries the heavy weight of being a Holocaust survivor. Mike, even in his nineties, clearly remembers fighting other kids in the 1920s and 1930s who misidentified his Arab looks and took him to be a cowardly Jew or a "wop." And similar to Will and Janice Crane, there was a generational gap between Mike and his mother, Rose. Mike kept school-yard altercations secret from his mother, knowing that his reaction—fighting back—would not have been to her liking. "I wasn't brought up in prejudice, and so my mother couldn't understand why I revolted from people attacking me for being a Jew, being a wop, being this, being that or the other. I thought I was the same as they were. I was just another human being. I didn't need that, and then they were, 'All Jews are cowards,' so some of them punched me, and those got punched right back, and that was all there was to it." Being misidentified by others can cause one's own identity to be a moving target. Mike, despite his Lebanese background, likes to joke that he is Jewish, given that his closest friends have always been Jewish and throughout his life he has been mistakenly identified as Jewish. This situation was facilitated by the fact that, where Mike grew up, the Lebanese community was largely made up of only his own siblings. Equally important, his mother did not require that he cling to a Lebanese identity; she never returned to Lebanon, nor did she insist that her children marry other Lebanese.

What is notable about the lunchtime interaction described above is that Mike and Sylvia are approached as elderly persons who hold valuable community knowledge, and they freely impart their wisdom. From this place of honor, they each willingly introduce a unique interpretive frame, which, for Mike, was informed by his mother.

VOICES

Ethnic and religious identities can shift. Individuals can carry conflicted identities, and identities may differ among close family members or over generations. The voices represented in this work are also divergent and dynamic. Although this work is dedicated to gathering women's tales,[5] my original intention was simply to chronicle the stories of Arab and Jewish store owners in Kentucky. But I soon realized that I was talking predominantly to men about men, as though they alone coordinated and negotiated their families' public lives. I even found that when women and their stories presented themselves, I tended to negate them. This became clear during an interview with Joe and Alberta Isaac, Teresa's uncle and aunt.

The husband and wife hailed from the mountainous eastern Kentucky community of Cumberland. Joe was Lebanese American, whereas Alberta was a "blond," as her husband described her. In transcribing their interview, I realized that I overlooked Alberta's incredible story of being a girl from the mountains who had married into a Lebanese family at a time and place where this was uncommon. The couple eloped (a bold act, considering that Joe's father had taken him to the Northeast specifically to meet Lebanese girls) and did not tell Joe's father they were married until after the fact. As Joe explained, "Yeah, I was the oldest son. Anyway, my father . . . had a theater in Whitesburg, so he had gone to Whitesburg. I told Mama that we were staying all night in the [upstairs] apartment. It was the first time. She knew that we were married. Nobody else knew. We were staying in this apartment, in my father's apartment. . . . So my father comes in from Whitesburg late at night, after the show, and was walking towards this apartment building he had, and my mother says, 'You can't go in there.' My daddy says, 'Why?' She said, 'Junior'—they called me Junior, 'cause I was named after my father—she said, 'Junior's in there.' 'So what's he doing in there?' 'He's in there with his wife.' Daddy turned around and went back to Whitesburg and didn't come back for a day or two." Joe's Lebanese father did not call his new daughter-in-law by name; instead, he labeled her "that girl," as he did with subsequent daughters-in-law. The couple eventually left the mountains to open a variety of businesses in central Kentucky. Joe recognized that his business ventures would not have been possible without Alberta. "We were in the rental real estate business, and no matter what I've ever been in, no matter what now—Burger Shake, steakhouse, real estate, dry cleaning business—my wife has been there doing everything with us. She has been like a backbone or a rock on everything we've ever done. If she'd been another kind of wife, we'd [have gotten] discouraged. I got discouraged coming down here [from Cumberland to Lexington]. We couldn't find a place. If she

Joe and Alberta Isaac. (Photo by Sarah Jane Sanders.)

had been a different kind of wife and not been supportive fully, we would have stayed in Cumberland. But every time we've done something, she has been fully supportive and worked hard. She's good stock."

Alberta's story is not chronicled here, in part because she is not Arab or Jewish. But her story, even as narrated by her husband, awakened me to the role of women in Arab and Jewish families. The image lingers of a secretly married couple, the new wife facing a displeased, strict, and foreign father-in-law. Equally embedded in the tale is the role of Joe's mother, who was a trusted confidante and ran interference between father and son. Others also alerted me to the important role women played.

Of her own accord, Janice Crane narrated her family's story, with her Lithuanian mother as the central figure. Janice, along with her sister, Betty Jean, recounted their mother's 1920s road trip from Lexington to Cincinnati and back, at a time when interstate highways did not exist and their mother had no driver's license. According to Betty Jean, "She was a pistol." Janice remembered that their mother's drive to Cincinnati "freaked everybody out, 'cause you took the train." Betty Jean then told the story: "There was some big holiday coming up, and her father needed dresses for the store, and didn't have anything, and he needed them. So she took a car, their car, and somebody went with her. They drove to Cincinnati so that she could buy dresses, and put them in the car and came back. Well, she never really had driver's lessons. In those days, I don't know that you even needed to have a license, and her brother had a store in Cincinnati at the time, and when he found out that she had driven from Lexington to Cincinnati, he was just, 'Oh my God. I don't know how she got there.' She did. She got the clothes and went back, and they sold them."

Renee Hymson, now in her seventies, had to execute creative domestic feats while raising her daughters and working full-time in the family store in the 1950s and 1960s. "I had help one day a week. I think the hardest part for a woman was probably [working] six days a week, and in those days, grocery stores were not open at night, and you had to cook at night. You couldn't go in and buy something already cooked. You had to cook it yourself."

Mike Rowady credited his mother's toughness for making sure that all seven of her children went to college, even though she was poor and caring for a sick and dying husband in the 1930s. As Mike said, "She was pushing to get ahead and behind us all the time."

Taking my cue from the people I spoke with, I center on women in this work. But even though I highlight women and their stories, men's narratives are not absent. In my past work about adoptive mothers, I ignored the fathers. This was perhaps a mistake, as if men and women were traversing separate universes. In the present work, men are included because the featured women belonged to families and communities that worked and lived together. In some cases, men offered their interpretations of female relatives who were no longer alive. Accordingly, part of the story is how men choose to portray not just themselves but also their mothers, grandmothers, and aunts. It may well be a rare occasion when men reflect on the influential women in their lives, and rich insights can be found in men's impressions of these women.

The voices included in this work are multiple not just because they are male and female; the men and women also speak out of different contexts. The age of the interviewees ranged from their forties to nineties. Although there is some intergenerational correspondence in the stories, the voices of young people (thirty and younger, a group represented by

Will Crane) are largely missing and deserve inclusion in any future work. The narratives shared in subsequent chapters reflect the situation of women raising families at a variety of times between the 1920s and 1990s, including contemporary women navigating both workplace and domestic demands. My grandmother, for example, tended to her family and to the family store in the 1920s and 1930s, when telephones were foreign devices. Her ninety-three-year-old son, Franklin Moosnick, explained the role of the telephone when he was young: "In those days—and this was not just us, it was everybody—the people were just not addicted to the telephone like they are now. You didn't call anybody unless you had something to say to them. You didn't call up just to kill time or to check in or anything like that. If you called, you called because you wanted to inquire about their health if they had been feeling bad, . . . but you'd never just call up so-and-so just to see how they were getting along. You rarely did that." Manar Shalash, in contrast, is decidedly of the modern electronic age. Her family is in the business of selling cellular phones, and she is able to work from home thanks to e-mail and instant messaging. "Yeah, thank God for technology with e-mails and MSN messenger. From the house, I can keep in touch with all the employees on my laptop. If I have a question, they'll answer it, so it really helps."

BUSINESS VARIETIES

Many of the businesses are long gone; others still exist and reflect contemporary habits, such as cell phone use. Some stores were treasured by the families that ran them. When asked, "How important do you think the store was to your family?" sisters Simone Salomon and Janice Brock responded in unison: "Everything. Everything." Simone continued: "It really was. In fact, the week when the store burned, it was like somebody had died. It was horrible. It took them [her parents] a long time to get over that." But the sisters had different degrees of affection for the family business: Simone loathed the store, whereas Janice, with the encouragement of their parents, carried on the business. "They tried," she said, and "they did convince me that if you didn't have your own business, you didn't have anything." For others, like Sawsan Salem, the business was just a brief and passing endeavor.

The role women played in the businesses also varied. Sarah and Frances Myers and Gishie Bloomfield, among others, were the forces behind their family businesses. Sylvia Green, in contrast, was distant from the business run by her husband and in-laws. "No, I didn't work in the store," she said. "Our agreement was that I would raise the children." But before Sylvia's maternal devotion, she was an accomplished saleswoman at a prominent central Kentucky department store. "It was in the newspaper [that] a Holocaust survivor was working at Wolf Wiles, so they [the customers] wanted to see what I looked like, and so they asked for me to wait on them. . . . The two years I worked, I won the first prize [for] the highest sales. . . . I got my picture taken free as a gift for [having] the highest sales." Clearly, business accomplishments can remain a source of pride, even if the businesses are long gone. Renee Hymson and Rose Marie Farah both married men with women's clothing stores and told of bringing color to their husbands' drab tastes and palettes. Rose Marie's husband ran "a department store for a while, but when I married him, it had just been a woman's shop, upstairs. Lord, there were baby clothes, all kinds of stuff from years [ago]. Licha [her husband] had fixed it up anew a little bit—lowered the ceilings and put carpet in and some new cabinetry. Of course, it was all with a man's taste, browns and golds. All the women came in during their lunchtime to see what I had in, and I did a pretty good job. I surely did bring up the wares a little bit—the style and all. Some of the young people, they're middle-aged now, they'll say, 'Oh, Miss Farah, I remember you,' and they tell me I was pretty and they say, 'You brought style to Carlisle.'" Some interviewees told me they held their unique talents as women out of reach of their husbands. Others offered business support only when they received domestic assistance. Nahil Natour said, "After my father-in-law died, my mother-in-law, she help me. She take care of the kids. I come [to the family grocery store] in the afternoon after I finish my cooking and cleaning and stuff like that. My husband take care of it in the morning. In the afternoon, it gets busy, that's why I come in the afternoon."

Whether working in the family store, tending to domestic chores, or overseeing community events, the women often had to manage multiple tasks. For some families, the juggling image also applied to the businesses themselves; in some cases, there was a never-ending assortment of entrepreneurial undertakings as families opened several businesses simultaneously or successively over time. Janice Crane's mother, for example, had Gigi's dress shop and then a general goods store in the 1960s. In the early to mid-1900s, many members of Janice's extended family had stores in central Kentucky. "At that time, a lot of our family had stores in the downtown [Lexington] area around here, like my grandfather had a store on Broadway. They all had stores. They had stores in Georgetown. Sam and Helen Levy had a store in Irvine. Ben Green had a store in Shelbyville." The practice of pursuing business opportunities with family members continues today. Manar Shalash and her husband, not completely satisfied with their previous business pursuits, decided to partner with her brother in a cell phone business. "We did grocery in the beginning," Manar said, "and then we switched to Subway. . . . My brother, he was using cell phones and pagers, so we were partners with my brother. Then he quit, and we kept on the business, so we're still in the cellular business. We've been doing it twelve years, and we've been happy with it."

The fates of the businesses diverged. Some families eventually closed their stores. My own family's store opened in 1924 and closed in 1958 as my grandmother got older and my father's and uncle's interests shifted away from retail. As noted earlier, my father apparently voiced an interest in expanding the store, only to be told by his mother that he was meant to be a professional, not a shopkeeper. Some families, like mine, opened their stores to get established in a new place, and once that was accomplished, they closed them; later generations were not shopkeepers. Salim Natour, in contrast, maintained his grocery store in Lexington. He reflected on the gender split in his family: "Maybe if educated, I wouldn't work in the grocery business. My boys, I tried to get them to go to college. They don't want to. And you can't force them to go to college. But my girls, they want[ed to go]; they finished. They went to college and have education. They have good jobs now. I had no choice. If I'm not a pharmacist or lawyer or doctor or something, the best I could [do was] make my living to take care of my family."

Some families let their businesses go as part of their progression toward professionalism. In other cases, family stores lost their viability in the changing business environment. Malls and large corporate buyouts altered consumer habits. Downtown areas were abandoned, and local businesses closed. Others adapted their businesses to changing family aspirations. In Teresa Isaac's family, later generations combined their professions with the family business; for example, they became attorneys devoted to the family mortgage company and real estate business. "Well, when my dad had a mortgage company here in town, we all worked for the mortgage company. So my aunt Barbara worked there, my aunt Mary Jo worked there, and my aunt Vicky worked there. My brother worked there, so we were all in the mortgage business. I was doing the title work, and my three aunts I think all had the realtor license, so they were doing the loan closings. There has always been a tradition of a family business." Others maintained their businesses by keeping up with the changing times. Manar and her husband, for instance, have chosen to run franchises. Finally, some businesses have changed surprisingly little over the years, such as the Burger Shake that has been handed down from generation to generation in Teresa's family. The pages ahead tell the story of the franchise store alongside that of the elegant dress shop that no longer exists.

This chapter has explained some of the complexities that inhabit lived stories. Lives are not uniform or easily delineated. In the next chapter, I start unraveling the stories of Arab and Jewish women in Kentucky and reveal their lives in detail.

2

PUBLICLY EXCEPTIONAL

THREE EXTRAORDINARY WOMEN are featured in this chapter. Howard Myers narrates the story of his aunts, Sarah and Frances Myers, from Hopkinsville, Kentucky. Who wouldn't be impressed with these two Jewish women? They brought big-city sophistication to rural Kentucky from the 1930s to the 1980s via their women's clothing store, Arnold's. They stood out among Jews and non-Jews alike in their community not just because of their success but also because of their remarkable personal lives: their longing for New York City, their failure to adhere to marital expectations, and Frances's struggle with depression, among other things.

Their story is juxtaposed with that of Teresa Isaac. Most people who are familiar with contemporary Kentucky politics know Teresa. She was mayor of the state's second largest city, Lexington, from 2002 to 2006. It is not her political policies and exploits, however, that make her exceptional (though perhaps they make her a hero to some people in the community and a villain to others). Rather, she is exceptional because she is a rare politician who openly embraces her own Arab American, Christian identity and reaches out to Muslim Arabs when most politicians would rather disassociate from all people and things Arab. Teresa's resolve stems from her upbringing in an entrepreneurial Lebanese family whose American life began in Appalachia in the early 1900s.

What ties Teresa Isaac to Sarah and Frances Myers? Similarities are not hard to find, even though Sarah and Frances were Jews who died years ago (Frances in 1983 and Sarah in 1990) and Teresa is now a fifty-something Arab American woman. Their families' stories are ones of "foreigners" who opened businesses in rural Kentucky and achieved exceptional success in their communities. Both families also had a knack for the dramatic. These women and their families did not fade into the community; instead, they became accomplished and significant public residents, carrying on their lives with panache.

Something more is nestled in their narratives. These three women didn't follow traditional gendered expectations—that is, the domestic sphere was not their primary focus. Sarah and Frances neither married nor had children. Teresa is the divorced mother of two grown children. Domestic obligations are not absent from their stories, but domestic life is not the focus of them. Men, though present in their lives, are secondary, and their domestic commitments pale in comparison to those of some of the women chronicled in later chapters. Sarah, Frances, and Teresa represent sophisticated women deeply committed to their broader families and communities and to aiding other women.

Sarah and Frances Myers
Arnold's
Hopkinsville, Kentucky

Howard Myers is Sarah and Frances's only living relative and the sole surviving voice on both his father's and mother's sides of the family—he was an only child and was in fact the only offspring of his generation. His father's five siblings had no children, and his mother's only sibling, Louis, did not marry or have children. Howard is the only one left to tell of his aunts' comfort, success, and yearning in Hopkinsville. His aunts' memories remain alive through him.

Sarah and Frances spent more than fifty years of their lives in Hopkinsville, located in western Kentucky. I accompanied Howard to Russellville, a small neighboring town that is part of the Greater Hopkinsville area his aunts knew. The difference between central and western Kentucky can be sensed immediately. Traveling from Lexington to Russellville, one leaves behind a mid-American city and enters the rural South, where expanded suburbia and any hints of Appalachian culture seem to disappear. Western Kentucky communities are more racially diverse, with larger populations of African Americans, than those in central Kentucky.

For residents of central Kentucky, the geographic focus is north toward Cincinnati, whereas for those in the western part of the state, it is south to Nashville, an hour and a half away. Hopkinsville is the county seat of Christian County and has a population of around 32,000. Historically, it is rural and agrarian; it is also home to Fort Campbell and thus has a strong military presence. It's not exactly a place one would expect to find Jews. Now that Howard has left Hopkinsville (he currently lives in Lexington), he believes there is only one Jewish family left in town, and that family moved to the community in the last four or five years. This is a change. Most of the longtime Jewish residents have died or moved away, and their children and grandchildren have settled elsewhere.

From the 1930s to maybe the 1970s, a small Jewish community existed in and around Hopkinsville. Howard estimates that perhaps 130 Jews lived within a fifty-mile radius of Hopkinsville in the 1930s. Jews were noticeable as shopkeepers. A synagogue stood in Hopkinsville from 1925 to 1977, and student rabbis from Cincinnati would arrive to provide religious guidance.[1] When the synagogue disappeared, these western Kentucky Jews had to travel to Nashville to own their Jewishness. Now it seems the Jewish community has largely faded into the past, as have their stores.

Howard closed his family's store, Arnold's, in March 1990, shortly after his aunt Sarah passed away. He waited to close the doors until after the last family member (other than himself) had died. It was a difficult chore, since many family memories lingered in the store. After Howard became fully involved in the family business in the 1980s, he and his aunt Sarah had generational differences; he was motivated by profit, she by an artistry of another era—one in which jeans were not fashionable. "In the sixties, my formative years, when denim became so popular, became so fashionable, and then people like Anne Klein came out with denim jeans, even your best designers, Sarah refused to have denim in the store because, she said, 'That's not fashion.' So only when I started [to get] more actively involved in the late seventies and eighties did we [sell jeans]. I was much more profit oriented, and whatever I could sell, I believed in buying, but she had those principles."

Some of Howard's own story emerged as he told his aunts', such as his business acumen and his own conflicted Jewish identity in Hopkinsville. "I think I faced some anti-Semitism, like, 'Are you going to Jew me down?' or 'You're a Christ killer, you killed Christ,' and some of that when I was six, eight, nine years old. I felt that. I felt different. The fact that on Yom Kippur, Rosh Hashanah I had to take off from school and people would ask. Being in the public schools and at Christmastime being asked to memorize Christian things—that [was] a conflict—and not wanting to be embarrassed about being Jewish. Or even if I could get permission to not do it [learn Christian things], that singled me out. I think it was those kinds of things, being raised in a Christian world." Although Howard tells of difficulties and conflicts that any Jew might face in any isolated setting, he prefers to create a grandiose image, distinguishing his aunts' story from that of other Jews of eastern European *shtetl* descent. "They were like these Hungarian Jews. They were very enthusiastic. They weren't hard core." Yet Sarah and Frances were not Hungarian; they were of Russian lineage, like so many other Ashkenazi Jews who settled in the United States.

Howard's aspiration for the splendid does not come out of the blue. Sarah and Frances exuded urban tastes and styles in an agrarian community. They stood out. But standing out in a rural community can cause some tricky situations. It might have been that the rural stage was too confining for them, or maybe appearances mattered too much. Whatever the cause, the result was an intricate backstage existence that involved financial strains, mental illness, and the interplay of family dynamics, Judaism, and relationships with other women.

There were hints that Sarah and Frances thought themselves too grand for Hopkinsville. Although they enjoyed enormous success there, they longed for more. For them, Hopkinsville was just "a place to live, a place for them to be, but I think if they had had their druthers, they would have made enough money to retire in a major city, with New York being their first choice." Sarah and Frances even gave Howard specific after-death directives: neither one wanted to be buried in Hopkinsville. "They always had plans for going for a bigger city." It's not surprising that Sarah and Frances Myers did not want to spend eternity in rural Kentucky, because Arnold's brought to mind the big city. "Arnold's was like a Sak's Fifth Avenue, but in this little country town. . . . People used to just marvel, and that's what I'm saying: my aunt Sarah dictated that she would not

Storefront of Arnold's in Hopkinsville, Kentucky. (Photo by Sarah Jane Sanders.)

lower [her standards]. Her store was a salon." As fate would have it, Sarah and Frances spent most of their lives in Hopkinsville and died there, but they were buried in Memphis, alongside their parents.

Sarah and Frances, along with some of the other women in their community, rebelled against their small-town lives. Sunday, the Myers sisters' only day away from the store, was devoted not to business or religious obligations but to cocktail parties by their swimming pool. While most of the community attended church, women gathered at the Myers house to drink and smoke long-stemmed cigarettes. Frances was the bartender. Howard recalled, "So there was this group of women, most weren't married, that hung out with them on Sundays, playing bridge, primarily drinking. . . . Sunday, there was always a party." Their Sunday cocktail gatherings were frequented by other prominent women in the community, women with "society ties." One of them was Katherine Peden, Kentucky's (and the nation's) first female commerce commissioner. Ms.

Peden, along with the "regulars," didn't fit prescribed models of femininity; some of them never married, focusing instead on work. Others had more difficult stories. Howard suspected that one woman may have expressed lesbian desires in another time and place. Another woman left her husband to be with a teenage boy, even though she was middle-aged when she fled. Women who ran from marriages and other relationships they no longer desired found refuge at Sarah and Frances's pool parties.

How did these two Jewish women, born to Russian parents and raised in Holly Springs, Mississippi, become urbane, sophisticated, and even rebellious? Howard suspects that his grandparents willed it. Sarah and Frances were born in 1903 and 1909, respectively. They were the only girls in a family of six children. Their parents had an upscale general store, and their father even entered into a business venture that involved purchasing farms in Mississippi—an enterprise that ended unsuccessfully. When their father became sick in the 1920s, he was sent to Johns Hopkins in Baltimore, a symbol, in Howard's mind, that the family wanted the best. "He died in the twenties. He had tongue cancer and went to Johns Hopkins, which was a huge deal back in those days, [traveling] from Holly Springs to try to get treatment."

Sarah and Frances moved to Kentucky at the advice of their older brother, J. D., in the hope of finding business success. "My uncle J. D. moved to Mayfield, Kentucky, in about 1933 and opened up a store. This was during the Depression, and as bad as things were in Kentucky, things were worse in Mississippi." Accompanying Sarah and Frances to western Kentucky were two other brothers who settled in Hopkinsville with them, Isaac Charles (known as I. C.) and Arnold. I. C. was Howard's father. The siblings opened Arnold's together, even though Sarah and Frances ran the business and made it a success, Sarah in particular.

Sarah tended toward the dramatic. "She taught speech in Mississippi, and I have some things that show she trained a couple Mississippi state champions in dramatic reading." She continued teaching speech and drama in Kentucky and could count among her high school students such future Kentucky dignitaries as Ned Breathitt, who became governor in 1963, and the aforementioned Katherine Peden. The latter crossed countless gender boundaries, and her work in Kentucky received national recognition, leading to her appointment to presidential advisory boards under Kennedy, Johnson, and Carter. Katherine was one of Sarah's life-long friends.

Sarah's dramatic talent was reflected in the accomplishments of her students and in her running of the store. "She treated the store like an artist, and some of my most vivid memories are watching her fold her garments or when she would open one up to display it, [it] was like a canvas in the store," Howard recalled. "The way she conducted herself and the way the store looked and so forth, it was like having someone to your home and being a hostess." Although Sarah could warmly welcome customers into the store, she was strong willed. "Sarah had this very dynamic personality. She was a very petite woman, about four foot ten. She never weighed more than probably ninety-eight pounds, but she was a real dynamo. She had a magnetic personality. She was just one of those assertive—well, no, she was still very southern and very feminine in her mannerisms. It wasn't that she was real aggressive and certainly not caustic by any means, very refined and so forth, but she had a very, very strong will and she was very determined. . . . She could be tough as far as being in business."

Part of Sarah's willfulness and determination manifested as a desire to dress women with care by ably matching the perfect dress with an individual woman, as only she could do. "We always had maybe a quarter of our better merchandise in the back, where people couldn't see it. The . . . woman would come on the sales floor, and Sarah would say, 'I have the perfect thing,' and she would go in the back. Unlike many of our salespeople, Sarah would usually bring out one thing, and it's amazing how often that worked. If that didn't work, she would go back. Many of our other salespeople would overwhelm the customer and come in with armfuls, and then give the person the choice. But Sarah had the mystique and the relationship with the women that said, 'We cater to our customers, and Miss Sarah knows.' And usually [a customer] never tried more than two or three things on, and [she] would be very pleased." Sarah catered to her customers by knowing them, their bodies, and the merchandise—but only quality merchandise from New York. "She just insisted that she have the latest fashion, and no one thought that a store like [Arnold's] could exist."

Sarah's commitment to the store and the family existed from the beginning. "When they started in the thirties," Howard said, "there was

Sarah Myers displaying hats inside Arnold's. (Courtesy Myers family.)

talk about Sarah getting up at five in the morning and coming down and stoking the fire, 'cause they had this in the retail store, this was in downtown Hopkinsville, 909 South Main, as a matter of fact." And even in those early years, the family was determined to bring extraordinary goods, reminiscent of New York, to western Kentucky. "The store from day one was considered a jewel in the community. This was before I was born, in the early 1940s; they always went to New York like six times a year to have the latest merchandise. They pushed the limits of how expensive the merchandise [was]. . . . My aunt Sarah was just absolutely determined to bring the highest fashion, the best." Part of the best included holiday displays that generated crowds on the sidewalk outside. "When it would be time for Christmas, they would hang drapes, and people would stand in line [to see the] mechanical sleighs from New York, and so it would be like an unveiling for the holiday season, and they would do this the day after Thanksgiving."

Business accelerated in the 1940s with the creation of Fort Campbell. This brought military luminaries to the store, General William Westmoreland's wife among them, and it sent Sarah overseas. "Their big success was when Fort Campbell was opened, which was in the mid or late forties. [At first] it was Camp Campbell, and then it became a full-fledged military post after World War II. The 101st was assigned there. The army was very formal in the forties and fifties, before Europe really recovered from World War II. As the soldiers or officers would be transferred to Europe, my aunt would ship merchandise [to them]. When [the army wives] would get to Europe, they couldn't find cocktail dresses and white gloves and all those things." In 1960 Sarah herself was summoned to Paris to dress Colonel Harry Critz's daughter on the occasion of her wedding. It is remarkable that Terry Critz sent for fashion help from Kentucky while living in postwar Paris. The *Nashville Tennessean* quoted Sarah as saying, "I feel like I'm carrying coals to New Castle." The same article recorded Terry Critz's commitment to Sarah, her longtime fashion consultant, despite having access to the fashion delights of Paris: "Since the Critz family has been residing in Paris, the bride-elect has attended showings at the famous houses of Christian Dior, Chanel, Patou and Balmain. She found their fashions 'extravagantly pretty.' But Miss Critz had always dreamed that when it came time for her wedding that Miss Myers would be her fashion-aide. And so her dream will come true."[2]

By 1960, Sarah's business mission to serve the whole woman was entrenched. "A big service that we did was the woman would be outfitted from head to toe—the hats to the gloves to the dress to the shoes—and all that would be coordinated, the handbag, the jewelry, and all that. But in those days, in the fifties, sixties, and seventies, that's what people liked. It wasn't you'd go buy a pair of pants here and a top there. It would be nothing for Sarah to work with a woman maybe four or five hours." An approach dedicated to the whole woman brought Arnold's success.

Success was signaled by the status of the women the Myers sisters outfitted, and their wares were often on display at public events in Kentucky and elsewhere. They provided Frances Breathitt with the dress she wore at her husband's inauguration as governor in 1963. Sarah outfitted Katherine Peden and traveled with her to Hawaii, where Katherine was installed as head of the National Federation of Business and Professional

Women's Clubs in 1961. "Katherine was a big woman," Howard recalled, "and she was considered one of the ten best-dressed women, and Sarah always outfitted her with hats, and so they were somewhat of a team."

Success coexisted with complicated familial relations. Certainly, Sarah was the mover and shaker in the family business, but her life did not exist apart from that of Frances and other family members. Sarah and Frances lived together in Hopkinsville; for a time, until her death, their mother lived with them too. "They were lifelong companions when it's all said and done, and they kind of catered to each another." Sarah chauffeured Frances around, seeing that Frances didn't drive, and they divided the household chores. "Frances took care of what's more perceived as the men's [work], some of the things. The division was that Frances was always the bartender when they gave their big parties. Frances always did the hors d'oeuvres. Whereas Sarah would do more of the cooking—not that she was a gourmet cook—but it was relatively straightforward, like steak, shrimp, hamburgers, but not casseroles or things where you're putting a lot of stuff together. It was more straightforward." They simply met each other's needs.

Sarah made sure that the house they built together in the 1950s had a pool to satisfy Frances's desire to swim, even though Sarah didn't know how to. They were committed to each other. Howard speculated that his aunt Sarah had several opportunities to marry, but every time she entertained the idea, she feared that Frances would collapse into emotional disarray and the store would falter. "Sarah had three or four opportunities probably to marry, and I'm saying this without being 100 percent sure I'm being accurate. It was like Sarah and Frances were married, and every time that Sarah would get involved on some level, Frances would assume that she was getting ready to leave. Frances would get into one of her depressions. It was like this passive-aggressive thing where it was very clear that Sarah was the matriarch, and Sarah would be on the verge of leaving and then realize [she couldn't because of] the store. . . . She never told me this, but my guess is that she didn't step out on her own because she felt that Frances was dependent on her, and [her brother] Arnold was dependent on her, and probably less so my father, but anyway, she had that sense."

Sarah worried about Frances's fragile emotional state. Although Fran-

of Hopkinsville. On the air she talked about fashion and civic happenings in an impromptu manner, fulfilling her dramatic training and desires. "Well, she would talk about fashion, but she would also . . . announce the various kinds of things that were going on in the community or she'd make comments, and if the Junior Auxiliary was doing their annual fundraiser, she would have somebody [on the show]. She would have a salesman to explain the newest fashions. She never would get into political things, but whatever was going on, like community announcements. She never had a script. She would just talk into the microphone. If she had someone to interview, she would play off of them, but for the most part, it was a monologue. She would get a garment and say, 'Now, I'm telling you about this A-line coat, that's in yellow, it has a big lapel with big black buttons,' and give a very detailed description of the garment. WHOP said it was one of their most listened to [programs]. It was an institution in itself, and so that was one of the things that was part of Arnold's image."

Some reconciliation between image and reality transpired when the first mall opened in Hopkinsville in the 1970s. The mall developers pursued and catered to Sarah and Frances as important local businesspeople who were needed to anchor the new development. "So the developers, who were from New York, basically gave Sarah and Frances a real sweetheart deal to kind of anchor the mall, so they gave them a really good deal. As a matter of fact, [the developers] paid for the renovations, which was probably putting [the store] into the shape that Sarah wanted. . . . They probably spent $150,000, $200,000 just for the interior of their store. Anything they did like that, they would have architects and designers from New York, and that's how they operated." Sarah and Frances, as treasured mall occupants, were allowed to maintain their old downtown ways, such as being closed in the evening and on Sundays—luxuries not extended to the other mall tenants.

In the mall, Sarah and Frances finally enjoyed the financial success and stability that outward appearances had led people to believe they had achieved long ago. "Where they made their real financial success is when they moved from downtown to the mall. Once they moved to the mall, they no longer had to borrow money to make their payments and, yes, because of the kind of merchandise, they were perceived as being wealthy because of dealing in that, but as far as accumulating a lot of wealth, they didn't. So that was basically when they really started accumulating wealth. . . . Sarah was sixty-nine years old when she made that move, and so a lot of the money that they made, she basically made when she was seventy years old and older. I remember very distinctly them paying off the mortgage on the house that they built in 1950 after they moved to the mall; it was something like '73. They burned it [the mortgage note] in our fireplace." It's not surprising that community members believed that Sarah and Frances had wealth before they did, because they worked hard to create such an image. The store was modern, and in representing urbane affinities and high-end tastes, it transcended rural life. The store in the mall was red and yellow, and according to Howard, "it was like something that would come out of *Architectural Digest.*"

Conscious of image, the sisters, and Sarah in particular, shunned public political participation. "They were careful, Sarah and Frances. They were always strong Democrats, but they tried to avoid being overtly political because of being in business. . . . Frances would be more support-ive [of Democratic candidates], but they would never have a yard sign in their yard." Like other whites in the community, they didn't disrupt racial taboos, even though they made small overtures to African Ameri-cans. Howard is proud of the fact that his aunts were the first to allow an African American employee to handle cash in a white Hopkinsville store. They also pursued a business enterprise with "Miss Mary," an Afri-can American woman who cooked and cleaned for them for many years. "They had this African American woman named Mary Jones," Howard recalled, "and Miss Mary must have come to work for them in the for-ties, and she worked six days a week, and probably only when she was in her seventies quit cooking the evening meal. I can remember Miss Mary being there, and . . . either her son-in-law would come pick her up or Sarah would take her home after the evening meal." The sisters' relation-ship with Miss Mary extended beyond that of employer and domestic helper. Sarah and Frances colluded with Miss Mary and her daughter, Holland, to create a black-oriented business enterprise at a time and place when this was frowned upon. "Holland was a cateress in Hopkinsville and fairly renowned with all these prominent families. Holland is the one who led a boycott of the local grocery store back in the fifties during the whole civil rights thing. Sarah and Frances helped support Mary and Holland.

We had always had African American trade, but we would take some of our merchandise and let Miss Holland and Miss Mary sell it out of their house. They had their own little trade among African Americans that didn't feel comfortable coming into a white store because of all those issues of trying merchandise on—not that I felt that my family felt those kinds of discriminatory things—but there were issues of trying a hat on . . . that went on in retail in the fifties and even through the sixties."

Female alliances existed in other realms as well. Sarah often expressed frustration at male manufacturers, distributors, and salesmen who thought they could take advantage of her because she was a woman. "With like a manufacturer, let's say, or a salesman that would . . . try to put pressure on her, she had a temper. She could let people know." Appreciating the position of women, Sarah and Frances nurtured their female employees, and virtually all their employees were female. Indeed, some of them worked in the store for twenty to fifty years and, in Howard's estimation, were like family. Even though the store was a comfortable environment for women to work in, Sarah expected a lot. Any employee who was not dressed to Sarah's liking would be sent home to change. Through these high expectations, the Myers sisters crafted future businesswomen and even allowed various women to live in their home for months at a time while learning the retail trade. They understood the importance of mentoring other women.

Their work on behalf of other women may have gone unnoticed by those at a distance. Likewise, non-Jews in particular may have been unaware of their complex relationship with their Jewishness. While Howard's parents played cards with the handful of other Jews in town, Sarah and Frances were more integrated, and their social lives included non-Jews. Sarah and Frances embraced being Jewish, though perhaps less so than did other family members and other Jewish families in town. Sarah even toyed with the idea of converting and joining the Episcopal Church, and she had her nose redone. The sisters, being celebrated community members, were simply more assimilated. Sarah spoke at churches, telling non-Jews about being Jewish. Sarah and Frances regularly attended religious services, and when services were not available in Hopkinsville, they traveled the hour or so to Nashville to express their Jewish faith. Like many other American Jews, they supported Israel by buying Israeli

Room in Howard Myers's home with portrait of Sarah Myers. (Photo by Sarah Jane Sanders.)

bonds. Frances even wore a star of David on her charm bracelet. And Sarah and Frances connected with other Jewish merchants by trading discounts. But they didn't act like other Jews, much to Howard's pleasure. They hung Christmas wreaths and declined to put Hanukkah lights in their windows, as Howard's parents were in the habit of doing.

Howard valued the extent to which his aunts were assimilated, especially in contrast to his mother's (the Sabel) side of the family, who never lost their overtly immigrant and Jewish ways. "My grandfather and grandmother [Myers] never spoke Yiddish in front of the children, and they tried to immediately completely assimilate. They claimed to be Jewish. They went to Memphis for the High Holidays. They knew they were Jewish, very pleased to be Jewish. When I say pleased, [I mean they] never ran from being Jewish. But a lot of the characteristics that, say, the Sabels had, they [the Myerses] had lost . . . , whereas the Sabels and all my cousins and family [on my mother's side], they definitely had the characteristics of immigrants. The way they dressed—plain, not real fashionable, or drab. They would say things [like], 'The *goyim* this and that.' So, yes, Sarah and Frances were taught, their parents emphasized for them to assimilate; that was a value that they had. They certainly passed that down to me. And that's the way they lived their lives in Hopkinsville." Being Jewish mattered to Sarah and Frances, but so did being elegant and sophisticated.

It's not clear whether being Jewish in rural Kentucky contributed to the mental illness that plagued the family. Frances's depression was noteworthy because it was an ongoing struggle; every four to five years she would have to be hospitalized when things became too overwhelming for her. In 1983, at age seventy-two, Frances took her own life. She was not the only member of Howard's family to do this. Five family members, mostly women, from both his mother's and father's sides committed suicide. His mother's brother, Louis, battled depression and required institutional care. "Louis always had a lot of mental issues. We had carried him up to Our Lady of Peace in Louisville a whole lot, so between Louis, my mother, and Frances, I dare say in my formative years that a year hardly ever went by where one of them wasn't being taken to Our Lady of Peace to deal with depression and [receive] shock therapy." Howard's mother and his aunt (by marriage) ended their own lives, as did his maternal grandmother, although he doesn't mention her here. "My mother, Frances, and Stella, who's not related to me by blood, and then Morris, one of my father's brothers (this was prior to me being born, like in the mid-1940s)" committed suicide. Mental illness clearly surrounded the family. Stella, Arnold's wife, was unlike the other family suicides; according to Howard's unsympathetic portrayal of her (as a mean, redheaded non-Jew), Stella was a hypochondriac who spent her time frequenting doctors and, in the process, developed an addiction to pills. The rest of the family, by contrast, self-destructed without the help of pills. At times, Howard links the pervasive depression in his family to being Jewish and suffering the social toll of being "different" in their isolated southern communities. More prominently, however, he attributes their mental illness to genetics.[3] Sarah and Frances acknowledged their family's problems with mental illness through public and civic actions, including their participation in the establishment of a mental health center in Hopkinsville.

Howard has more to say about Sarah and Frances, and there may be additional interviews to enlarge his aunts' stories even more. But from these brief pages dedicated to Sarah and Frances Myers, it is clear that they were exceptional women who balanced public success with private conflicts.

TERESA ISAAC
THE CUMBERLAND AMUSEMENT COMPANY
CUMBERLAND AND LEXINGTON, KENTUCKY

Teresa's life may lack the emotional intrigue of Sarah and Frances's, but like that of the Myers sisters, the Isaac family's tale is one of success. Their story involves Lebanese immigrants establishing themselves as elegant theater owners in eastern Kentucky and achieving business eminence, allowing later members of the family, including Teresa, to pursue political careers.

Most Kentuckians know Teresa Isaac as the former mayor of Lexington. At first glance, she appears, like most politicians, to singularly represent herself. Upon closer examination, it's clear that her political career is rooted in her family, the family business, and her Arab American identity.

Prominent in the family narrative are legends of enterprising Lebanese immigrants making their home in the Appalachian community of Cumberland, Kentucky. Almost as significant are later generations that have assimilated to the point of disassociating themselves from an Arab identity, preferring to be just American. But Teresa is not one of them. Instead, she owns and negotiates her Arab American identity in the contemporary Kentucky context, and she does so publicly. Unlike Sarah and Frances Myers, Teresa is manifestly political. She does not recoil from controversy. She openly attempts to bridge the gap between Arab Christians and Muslims in Lexington. Couching herself in national and international Arab contexts, she associates with the Arab American Institute in Washington, D.C., and monitored the first elections in Palestine in 1996 as an international State Department educator. She may even find herself negotiating the desires of Jews, for she is sometimes misidentified as Jewish (or Muslim). Teresa can count Jews among her longtime loyal political supporters, even if her political foes try to pit Jews against her. "When I ran for mayor the first time," she said, "flyers got put on the cars at the synagogue and temple that said I was a terrorist, and so the Arab American community was going to do a press conference and say that that wasn't true. Then actually the Jewish community did a press conference and said it wasn't true, so it was very nice. They [her opponents] were [also] saying that I was Muslim. . . . There is nothing wrong with it [being Muslim], . . . so you don't want to slam Muslim people by saying, 'I'm not Muslim,' but I'm not Muslim."

Let's be clear: Teresa is not the typical Arab American politician. And most Christian Arab Americans, politicians or not, distance themselves from Muslims. As noted earlier, Teresa also identifies with the mountains of Kentucky, even though it has been years since she lived in the eastern part of the state. Despite her busy schedule, she makes an effort to maintain ties to the region. "Anytime that they [people from eastern Kentucky] have asked me to come back—like I was the commencement speaker for Southeastern Community College—or anytime they've asked me to come and help them with grants like the Housing Council—we actually wrote a grant for Harlan County—anytime that I can help eastern Kentucky, I try to."

I'm not the only one who has noticed Teresa's distinctive political style. The State Department has sent her around the world to represent the United States. "I have trained police chiefs and elected officials for the State Department in Chile, Argentina, South Africa, Namibia, Pakistan, and Uganda." Her work in Kentucky and worldwide has also captured the attention of Arab Americans. James Zogby, for instance, the founder of the Arab American Institute, was amazed to find an Arab American politician willing to own her identity and reach out to Muslims and Christians alike. Perhaps most of all, he was surprised to find her in Kentucky. As Teresa explained, "I know in the old country probably the Christians were more persecuted by the Muslims then, and so people are always amazed that I will reach out to the Muslim community here, but to me, the 'Arabness' supersedes the religion, and we should be able to work together. So, for example, when Jim Zogby comes to town, if he wants to talk about Arab issues, I will actually get the Muslims and Christians together at one dinner so he can talk to them. And he says that in very few communities does that happen, where you can get the Muslim and the Christian groups together."

Teresa has established herself in the national Arab American community and beyond. In 2007 she received the Najeeb Halaby Award for public service from the Arab American Institute Foundation. The award is named for the late father of Jordan's former Queen Noor. Teresa was also one of thirty U.S. representatives sent to the U.S.–Islamic World Forum held in Doha, Qatar, in 2007. The purpose of the forum, according to Teresa, "was to bridge the gap between young people in the Muslim countries and the United States, and to start using social media to interact with people in the United States and people in the Muslim countries. So I did a session with young people from Muslim countries. How do you use Twitter, how do you use Facebook to interact with each other and to promote friendship? So if you look on my Facebook account and the friends that I have, you'll see all these people from over there."

No doubt, Teresa embraces a nuanced identity as a female Arab American politician and representative who hails from the mountains of Kentucky. She can even confuse fellow Arabs elsewhere. When Teresa monitored the Palestinian elections in 1996, she puzzled the residents of Palestine. "The people in Palestine, they were looking at me and they were like, 'You look just like us, but what is that accent?' I'm like, 'It's from Kentucky.' And they would be [thinking], what on earth is an Arab doing

Teresa Isaac with other women in Pakistan. (Courtesy Teresa Isaac.)

in Kentucky? They were just mystified that an Arab from Kentucky had come to monitor the first Palestinian elections. I just always told them that it [Kentucky] reminded my grandparents of the mountains of Lebanon. . . . No one's ever told me that, but I thought it has to . . . remind them of home a little bit, but I don't know if that's the reason or not." Teresa works from the belief that Arab American Christians with eastern Kentucky roots can be unique peacemakers; she even sees Christian Arabs as a bridge between Jews and Muslims. In her estimation, Arab American Christians share ethnicity—or "blood"—with Muslims, and they share the Old Testament with Jews. She approaches her State Department assignments as efforts to improve the image of the United States abroad. "It's supposed to put a better face on America, our foreign policy, because I think sometimes people in these countries [do not] have a great perception of us, and I think it's supposed to show a better side of America."

What is curious about Teresa's global travels is that they do not cause her to feel more worldly or sophisticated than other Kentuckians; instead, they make her feel more attached to them. Even when she is overseas, far from Kentucky, she manages to uncover Kentucky connections. For

instance, Teresa knows a police officer in Versailles, Kentucky, with relatives in Qatar. "He met me at the McDonald's in Versailles," she said, "and
he texted his parents while we were sitting there, and he gave them all
the information [about] when my plane would get to Doha, so his parents were there when I landed in Doha. Who would think that someone
in Versailles, Kentucky, would have relatives in Doha and that I would
find them?" It was the same thing in Uganda, where Teresa traveled to
train "one hundred and twenty candidates and elected officials for their
elections, which were February 18 [2011]. . . . I would go into all of the
quadrants [of Uganda], and sometimes we would have to drive like eight
hours to get to a place and the roads would be very bad. They would just
be dirt roads. You knew that you were going to be gone all day driving
there." Teresa knows a young man from Uganda who's a hip-hop artist in
Lexington. "His mom is one of the most renowned HIV/AIDS doctors
over there. I met her, [and] we had dinner in Kampala." People at the State
Department were amazed: "How do you always find a Kentucky connection, no matter what country you're in?"

Opportunities have come to Teresa because she embraces her identity
as a Catholic Arab American from the mountains of eastern Kentucky,
and she recognizes her lucky fate: "Who would have thought a girl from
Harlan would go to Uganda?" Like many others, she could have let her
Arab American identity lapse. Indeed, owing to her family's success and
prominence, it would have been easy for her to cast aside her family's
immigrant roots and present herself as simply American. Why does she
claim her roots, whereas other Arab Americans do not? Discrimination
might play a part. Fresh in Teresa's memory are her mother's experiences having a Lebanese father and a white mother in Roanoke, Virginia.
"When my mom was little in Roanoke, there was a pool for black people
and Arabs, and a pool for white people. So when she'd go swimming with
her dad, she'd go to the black, Arab pool, and when she'd go swimming
with her mom, they would go to the white pool. She spent her childhood
this way, thinking, 'How can I be in one pool one day and then another
pool the next day, just depending on the skin color of my parents?' But
that's how it was." Later, Teresa's mother realized that this was discrimination, but while growing up in Virginia, she "just thought, 'This is the
way it is.' She said, 'I never thought to challenge it or say this is wrong.'

She said, 'Now I know that it was wrong,' but at the time, she just thought this is the way the world is. Yeah, I'm like, 'Mom, why didn't you ever say anything? This is unfair. This is wrong.' And she just said, 'We didn't think that way. We just thought this is the way it is.'"

Teresa may be motivated by her mother's inaction in the face of injustice. It is also likely that she doesn't have the option of discarding her heritage. Teresa has dark, Arab, ethnic looks. Out of the seven children that her Lebanese grandparents raised in Cumberland, only Teresa's father married someone who is also Lebanese American. Intermarriage was and is the norm, and grandchildren and great-grandchildren range from blond to dark. Teresa recalls disparaging remarks—being called "sand nigger" and "black"—as a nine-year-old who had just left the mountains with her family to build a new life in central Kentucky. There was confusion over her dark looks, and the question, "What are you?" greeted her in Lexington, especially when her skin darkened in the summer sun. Certainly, Teresa has faced moments in the past when her ethnicity caused negative reactions, but ultimately, she said, "I do feel that for the most part it has been neutral."

Despite a preponderance of neutral reactions, Teresa relates to people of color and is aware that her easy association with African Americans stems from her own passing encounters with discrimination. "Just that experience of growing up and knowing what discrimination is like, I think you can relate." Teresa may feel a connection with African Americans, but she is often mistaken for a Jew. "Well, people always assumed I was Jewish because of the name, and I would say, 'I'm a Catholic Arab.' And they would be absolutely stunned because they had no idea that I was Arab. . . . With the last name Isaac, they just assumed it was Jewish." Maybe Teresa is one of those modern ethnic and racial beings who confuse others. For example, the actor Ben Kingsley is taken to be Indian one moment and is convincingly Jewish the next, while it may be that he is actually both Indian and Jewish. The confusion over Teresa's racial or ethnic makeup appeals to the State Department. "I think that's why the State Department uses me," she said, "because I can blend in. When I'm in Chile and Argentina, they think I'm like them; when I'm in Pakistan, I can dress up like them and go out and nobody can really tell, so I think I can blend."

Teresa Isaac. (Photo by Sarah Jane Sanders.)

Her chameleon looks have brought both advantages and disadvantages. Her looks and her name align her with her past. Unlike some of her cousins, who are products of intermarriage, both her mother and her father transmitted their Lebanese background to her. "I was getting a double dose, and maybe they [her cousins] were getting a single dose, because on both sides of my family, when we would have get-togethers, I was getting the Arab food, the Arab dance, the Arab culture." She vividly recalls going to *Haflis,* or Lebanese social gatherings, while growing up: "So you would go to these meetings, which were mainly social events really, and you would see people who looked exactly like you—your nose, your hair, your eyes, your skin color—and it was just nice getting to know other people whose grandparents had come from the same place your grandparents had come from. But it wasn't . . . very political. It was mainly social. Matchmaking was going on, and people were finding other people, becoming friends with them. And then they would meet at other conventions, but it seemed much more social to me than political." Today, she still reconnects with friends from the *Haflis* in the more political setting of the Arab American Institute. "We keep friendships from then, and the Arab American Institute now has a lot of meetings which are much more political, and so at some of those meetings I will see people that I had seen earlier at the social meetings, but these meetings . . . are mainly political, focused on what can we do for America to have a better image in the rest of the world, that kind of thing."

It's pretty obvious that Teresa's resolve to be overtly Arab American and to participate in, not shun, difficult conversations has a lot to do with her family and its deep ties with Kentucky. Teresa is part of a large, tight-knit family. "People are amazed sometimes when I tell them how close I am with my cousins or my second cousins or my third cousins. Other people say, 'I hardly speak to my sister.' I don't understand that lack of closeness in other people's families; I assume that everybody comes out of that tradition where you are close to your aunts, your uncles, your grandparents, your great-aunts. I used to take that for granted, and now I'm like, 'Wow, that is really something special.' I think mountain people have [it], and I know Arab people and other ethnic groups have it too, but I just think it's important to have those kinds of ties. It's important to your kids to pass on stories. I swear, I feel sorry for people that don't have that."

Even when Teresa is in distant lands on her State Department trips, her family is on her mind. She brought rocks from Uganda for a sick aunt who believed that rocks have numinous powers, and she's aware that her parents worry about her when she's overseas. "My parents aren't crazy about me doing it," she admitted. "My parents are always very worried, but it's always okay." And she knows to be prepared for her parents' post-trip questioning: "Did you go to mass?" To a certain extent, she tries to fulfill their desire for her to be a good Catholic, whether at home or abroad. "I did watch church TV [in Uganda]," she said. "And I bought a nativity—that counts. And I went to a Catholic school, and there was a Virgin Mary in the middle of the school yard. That counts. I think that was on a Sunday." About her parents' focus on religion, she noted, "My parents just wanted me to be married in the Catholic Church, which I did, so that made them happy. So it is the religion that matters more, not so much the Lebanese."

Teresa does not disassociate from her family; rather, she situates herself in their lives and history. A host of familial characters, both men and women, from the past and present speak to Teresa. Her story is an extension of her large family, not separate from it. Her father, who served as mayor of Cumberland in the 1960s, inspired her to enter politics. "I can remember going around with him and shaking hands, 'cause my mom was pregnant at the time, so I got to go to a lot of things with my dad because she was at home getting ready to have the baby. So that kind of exposed me at an early age to the shaking hands and the handing out everything, and it was fun to be doing that." Teresa's children may keep the family mayoral tradition alive. There is a family picture of Teresa, her parents, and her children in which her father (the first mayor in the family) is holding up one finger and Teresa (the second mayor in the family) is holding up two fingers. "My kids, they want to do a picture with one, two, and three."

A whole cast of men and women in Teresa's family has influenced her. Among the men, in addition to her father is her grandfather on her father's side, Joseph Isaac Sr. Joe Senior stirred the whole family. He was not unlike the Myers sisters in terms of his dramatic presence in the family and in his rural Kentucky town. Mr. Isaac was one of those famous family characters, and his presence remains with his children and his grandchildren, particularly with his eldest son and namesake, Joe Isaac Jr., Teresa's uncle. "Uncle Joe" is in his eighties. As the eldest son of the original Lebanese family, he is the keeper of the family's stories and memories, and he owns the role. "I maintain the e-mails of all our nieces and nephews," he told me, "and any time somebody has a birth or something happens, I'll send an e-mail to everybody in the family, forty, fifty people." Teresa, like other family members, knows to turn to her uncle for artifacts from the past, "because Uncle Joe saves everything." She directed me to him as a way to extend her own story.

I met Joe and his wife, Alberta, in their Lexington home. Their modest lifestyle conceals the fact that one daughter is a judge in town and their son is an executive with an NBA team. Another daughter, along with a cousin, runs the Burger Shake, the first fast-food restaurant in town, which Joe and his cousin founded in 1957. It is now a Lexington institution, but in the early days, it required plain hard work and wasn't necessarily what Joe Junior's father had in mind for his educated son. "When I graduated," Joe said, "I graduated in business at UK [University of Kentucky], and I'd been to VPI [Virginia Polytechnic Institute], Milligan, and Rice. I'd had three years of aeronautical engineering courses, and I built a hamburger stand. My father called me the most educated hamburger person in Fayette County." His dad's opinion mattered. Joseph Senior was the entrepreneurial genius who established the family in eastern Kentucky with a theater business. Joe Senior and his wife, Alene, came to this country at a young age. "They came over, let me see, Mama was five," Joe Junior recalled. "They came over in like 1905 or 1906. Both my parents came over then. They didn't know each other or anything. They met while they were in this country. Both were full-blooded Lebanese. Back then it was Syria, because Lebanon was part of Syria."[4] Little is known about their lives in Lebanon.

Teresa's family memory begins in rural Appalachia. Her grandmother's expansive family settled in Mullens, West Virginia, and her grandfather's set down in Norton, Virginia. There, in coal country, they were peddlers and shopkeepers. As a married couple, Teresa's grandparents remained in Appalachia, in Cumberland, Kentucky, where they raised their seven children and established the family theater business. They were the only Lebanese family in town and one of the few that were not coal miners. Teresa reflected on the relationship between her family and the miners: "We were the entertainment for the coal miners, and that was how we made all our money. We were the white-collar workers, and they were the blue-collar workers. That's exactly how it was, but everybody was still friends and everybody was respectful of each other, and I don't think anybody was looking down on anybody. I certainly don't remember looking down on people that were miners."

The dominant figure in the family was Teresa's grandfather, Joe Senior. He was an entrepreneur who tried his hand at multiple schemes. As Joe Junior explained, "Daddy moved to Cumberland, Kentucky. It was called Poor Fork when he went there, and he opened a dry goods store. I'm getting ahead of myself. He opened a theater in Norton, Virginia, . . . him and this other guy. My daddy was a showman. He knew how to advertise and get newspaper space and everything, and he got competition, and these two guys kept lowering their prices till both of them went out of business. There was just too much competition, so he went to Cumberland and opened a dry goods store and later converted it to a theater, the Cumberland Theater. He did well in the theater business over there."

The theater business hardly resembled Joe Senior's initial entrepreneurial forays. According to a famous family story, when he couldn't get a loan because he was "foreign" (and perhaps because he was involved in the risky theater business), he opened his own bank. Teresa tells the story this way: "Our grandfather would try to get bank loans when he first came here, and they wouldn't give him a loan. So he would save up enough cash . . . and then do it [whatever business enterprise he had in mind] anyway, but do it with cash. And then he started his own bank. He started Cumberland Deposit Bank in Cumberland, so I think there has been [an attitude of] this is where I am, this is where I'm going, [and a] stand my ground kind of thing." And her grandfather did.

After opening the first theater in Cumberland, Joe Senior eventually had a chain of ten or eleven theaters, according to his son. Similar to the Myers family, Mr. Isaac relied on New Yorkers for design work. Joe Junior recalled, "He built the Novo Theater, which at the time was one of the most modern theaters in Kentucky. He got this New York architect to come in to draw a plan [and] to come down and supervise the construction of the theater, and it was really beautiful." According to Teresa, the intention was that each of the seven children in the family would eventually have a theater. "As each theater would make more money, then they'd reinvest and build another theater until there was enough for each kid to run one theater. The theaters did in fact spread. He [Joe Senior] bought a theater in Whitesburg. We had a theater in Appalachia, Virginia. We had two theaters in Pikeville, Kentucky. We had a theater in Harlan, Kentucky, at one time."

In the process of initiating and expanding the business, Mr. Isaac, like the Myers sisters, imported big-city sophistication to small-town Kentucky. His sound system, Joe Junior recollected, was outstanding. "He brought a Western Electric sound system. He had one of the best sound systems around. . . . People would come in . . . to come test your sound and your tubes and everything, and they would always compliment him on his sound." The infrastructure was not the only sophisticated aspect of the Isaacs' theaters; the acts and the films they showed could be risqué (at least by Catholic Church standards). "Now, *The Outlaw,* with Jane Russell, was a movie that the Catholic Church [disapproved of]," according to Joe Junior. "My brother was working at the theater, [and] I was working at the other theater, and the priests came down and talked to my father: 'Do not run *The Outlaw*.' It was outlawed by the Church. They said, 'You can't run it.' Daddy said, 'What will you do if we run it?' He [the priest] said, 'I'll excommunicate [you].' And Daddy says, 'Well, I tell you what. On the day we run it, I'll send my son Junior up there. He's a Baptist.' But we ran it, and nothing happened." Mr. Isaac handled the situation with élan.

Resolve also infused Joe Senior' self-presentation, including the way he dressed. His formal attire was memorable, and both Teresa and Joe Junior spoke of it. Teresa remembers that her grandfather was always dressed in a suit and had a hat adorning his head. Etched in her memory are the boxes from Slaughter's Men's Store (perhaps a Jewish-owned enterprise) in which her grandfather's suits were imported from Daytona Beach, Florida. As a child, she supposed that her grandfather slept in his suits, because she never saw him in anything else. Joe Junior had similar recollections of his father. "My father wore a clean white shirt every day, and he'd come home to his relaxing clothes. He would take off his coat and put on a smoking jacket. He was still formally dressed. I never saw my father's legs until he bought a place in Daytona and I saw him in shorts."

Joe Senior, always properly attired, expected a lot of his children and grandchildren: it was a given that family members would participate in the business. Children, grandchildren, and in-laws worked in the theaters and even lived behind or next to them. Teresa worked in the theaters as a child and recalls getting her very own stock in the company. "It was called Cumberland Amusement Company, that was the umbrella corporation, and I had stock from the Cumberland Amusement Company from when I was a baby. We all got stock in the company." It was a group effort.

Joe Senior loomed so large in the family and in the community that any recollection of discrimination is mostly absent from Teresa's and Joe Junior's stories. The family had social standing, and when I asked about possible difficulties, Joe Junior responded, "We had so little of that, it's not worth mentioning. We never felt [it]. Well, you have to remember our position in the community was very big, [being] in the theater and people coming to the show, so we were on a good level to start with." Theatergoers, for instance, understood that Mr. Isaac had rules. "My father was very strict about keeping the theater quiet, kids not crying, people don't put their feet on the seats, and everything. So when he would walk down the aisle—the theater's packed full, it's Sunday—he'd walk down the aisle, and you could hear people whispering, 'Here comes Mr. Isaac.' Feet would come off the seat and everything. He'd walk around and make everything just right."

Mr. Isaac, as president of a bank and a member of the Rotary Club, was community minded. He was also active in the war effort during World War II. "Daddy was very patriotic," Joe Junior noted. Teresa said the same thing about her grandfather and observed that he steers her even now. "My grandfather gave me a real sense of patriotism and duty, which I think guides me today. I think my grandparents and Richard Dawahare's grandparents were very big on public service. . . . We chose to come to this country, and this country has given us so much opportunity for education, to have a business, and so we have an obligation to give back. I think that's been very much passed down through my family and . . . through Richard's family too, 'cause when you . . . choose to come to a place to have a better life, and then you *have* a better life, you feel like you have an obligation to give back."[5]

The Isaacs' love of their eastern Kentucky community still reverberates today. Teresa counters the stereotype of Appalachians as mountain people who accept only their own and shun "outsiders," like her family. "People always treated our family nice, but now I know [that] when my dad ran for mayor in Cumberland, there were some people that would use the 'N word' toward him and say that he was an 'N.' I can remember that happening, but he won, so most of the people, that must not have bothered them, because they knew he was Arab. And Willy Dawahare, the same way in Hazard. He was mayor of Hazard at the same time that my dad was mayor of Cumberland, so the people there had to accept them, knowing they were Arab. To me, that's a good thing that mountain people were that accepting, 'cause most people paint a stereotype of mountain people as not being accepting." Life in Appalachia was good for the Isaacs, as independently confirmed by two generations—Joe Junior's and Teresa's.

Appalachia gave Teresa's family a sense of self and place and also granted them the financial resources to pursue other options. "The money from the theaters is what allowed each of the kids to move here [to Lexington] and invest in the real estate business," she said. That, in turn, "enabled the next generation to go to college, to go to law school, to do whatever we wanted to do, because of what our grandparents did and passed that wealth on."

When economic realities shifted in the late 1950s, Joe Junior knew it was time to leave Cumberland. "We kept the books for all the theaters, and I could see the level of admissions going down—slightly, but going down. I was the oldest, so I thought, well, I'll get out." In the late 1950s, Joe and a cousin led the way out of Appalachia. Brothers and sisters followed them to Lexington in the 1960s and 1970s. Outside of Appalachia, the Isaac family did not carry any weight. By 1957, Joe was married and had young children. Like so many military veterans, he was hoping to land a position at a solid corporation. Yet, despite his college education and his other qualifications, Joe did not succeed. "Before we came down and went into business, I wrote to IBM, GE. I wrote to several big corporations and sent a résumé, everything. I sent out fifty letters—nothing. I didn't get one answer. . . . I'm a business person, an engineering person, I'm a perfect type for these people. Nothing. But [now] I'm thankful, 'cause I never would have gone into business for myself, which is much better. But it is amazing. I guess after the war, veterans were coming back, they didn't need people, or maybe I asked for too much money back then. I asked for $10,000 a year. I don't know, in 1957, that would be like $60,000 or something now." Hidden in Joe Junior's account is the slight intimation that discrimination might have been the problem. Was it his Jewish-sounding name that blocked opportunities? Irrespective, in 1957 Joe and his cousin, along with their families, opened the first fast-food restaurant in Lexington: the Burger Shake.

The remainder of the family followed from eastern Kentucky and opened real estate and mortgage financing businesses. The family has stayed together in Lexington because, for the Isaacs, business speculation was and continues to be a family endeavor. Teresa explained the setup in her father's mortgage company: "What I did for the family business was in my private law practice. I was doing the real estate closings. So every-body, whatever their area was, they just helped with the family business." Similar to so many immigrant families who merged kinship and business, their tale is one of success, though perhaps not extraordinary success. Likewise, Teresa's political career is predicated on familial support in Lex-ington because, in her estimation, a political campaign is analogous to a family business. Politics is "like the family business," she said. "It's a con-tinuation of that. The whole family gets into it [her political campaigns]. . . . You've got to have your family's support; it's really important to me to have that."

The need to be fearless often comes up in conversations with Teresa, because she says it's a requirement for entering politics. And there are plenty of folks in her family who have demonstrated fearlessness, includ-ing her uncle Joe. The story of Joe's defiance of his father when he eloped with Alberta, a blond, non-Lebanese woman from the mountains, is a family legend (see chapter 1). As Teresa said, "Everybody knew that story." According to Joe, the day after he and Alberta secretly got married, "my father took me up to the Northeast to meet some Lebanese girls or Syr-ian girls. They were nice, but I had a blond, and that's what I wanted. The Lebanese girls were like my sisters. . . . They looked like my sisters. Later on, he probably thought that something was wrong with me because I wasn't connecting with any of the girls up there because I'd already got married to Alberta." Joe Junior was the first in the family to intermarry, but in the end, only one of Joe Senior's children married an Arab American—namely, Teresa's father.

Even though she was Arab American, Teresa's mother still had to meet her father-in-law's standards of acceptability. "I know the story about how he grilled my mom," Teresa said. "When my mom and my dad got married, my mom thought she was going to dinner with my grandfather *and* my grandmother, but it was just my grandfather. . . . He grilled her about what her intentions were, and she was just a kid. She was just like seventeen, and my grandfather scared her to death. My grandfather was very particular about who came into the family, but at least my mom was Lebanese, so he wasn't as hard on her as he was on the blonds. She had the right hair color to be in the family. He was very hard on the blonds."

Both Teresa's mother and her aunt Alberta adapted to their father-in-law by learning how to cook Lebanese food from their mother-in-law, Alene. Teresa described her this way, "Oh, [she was] not stern at all. Not stern at all. They [her grandparents] were a case of opposites attract. There was nothing stern about her, nothing." Teresa gives the impression that her grandmother enthralled others. "My grandmother Alene was enchanting, and she was so much fun to be around." Alene was the light counterpart to her steely husband. Money and business were not her concerns, and she quietly—or not so quietly—rebelled against her husband's rigorous attachment to financial precision. Joe Junior recalled, "Daddy was president of the bank, and Mama would get these overdrafts all the time, and Daddy would get on her and say, 'Look, this is embarrassing to me.' Well, back then, they didn't charge anything. They just overdrafted, and Daddy put in some more money. So one time they got into this fuss, and Daddy kept saying, 'You're spending too much,' and Mama said, 'No I'm not. You don't put enough money in the bank.'" Alene also fudged it when her husband interrogated her about food purchases. "She would never tell Daddy what she paid for food because she'd buy steaks, and Daddy would say, 'How much is it?' She'd always lower the price a dollar when she told him."

In Teresa's estimation, despite her grandmother's distance from the financial side of the family business, Alene was the one who kept people coming back to the theaters. "She worked in the business too, but, I guess, typical of that time, he [Joe Senior] didn't discuss any of the business with her. She probably could not have told you how the theaters were doing or what the balances were or anything like that, but she was the one that would greet the customers, and she was what kept them coming back. She was much more concerned about customer satisfaction, and he was much more concerned with the bottom line and the dollars. She had the soft touch and was just congenial with people." Alene was admired in the community both for her kind demeanor and for her extraordinary beauty. "I think that everybody in Harlan County thought that my grandmother and her sisters were just beautiful," Teresa recalled. "When her sisters would come to visit in Harlan County, they would all know that the Thomas girls were in town. . . . Apparently, all the boys in town were in love with them. They were very striking."

Alene can be counted among Teresa's familial role models. "She was an actress. She was in all the plays in her high school and her community, so I think the ones of us that ended up in law, that a lot of that 'drama' comes from her—being able to go into a courtroom and not being afraid of public speaking, I think that comes from her." Teresa is not the only one in the family to admire her grandmother. One of Teresa's cousins, who is named for Alene, keeps their grandmother's spirit alive by prominently displaying Alene's jewelry, clothes, and other treasures in her home, thereby honoring and testifying to their grandmother's style and elegance.

In addition to her grandmother, Teresa turns to her mother, aunt, and great-grandmother for inspiration. She honors these women partly because of their resolve, but also because she is keenly aware of the gendered roles in the family that consigned the women to the kitchen and the men to the dining room. Thanksgiving in Virginia remains a vivid memory for Teresa. "Thanksgiving was at my grandparents' in Roanoke, Virginia, and there was a huge Arab community there. When they would have Thanksgiving dinner, the men would be in one room, and the women would serve them; the women would eat later, after they served the men. That just used to irritate me to no end. I would always tell my mother, 'I'm going to go in and sit down.' And my mother would always say, 'Oh, you'll give your uncle Abner a heart attack if you do that,' so I never did. I never went in and sat at the men's table." According to Teresa, her mother taught her to choose her battles wisely. Her mother did not allow Teresa to disrupt the cultural status quo at Thanksgiving, but her mother challenged gendered practices elsewhere.

Teresa Isaac's aunt Barbara, who recently passed away, under a family photo displayed prominently in Teresa's cousin's home. (Photo by Sarah Jane Sanders.)

Despite having five children, Teresa's mother returned to the sport she loved, basketball, as a referee. "She refed high school basketball in Kentucky in '75, '76, '77," Teresa said with admiration. "The whole time I was in law school, she was refing basketball, and I thought that's amazing that she would do that. She had won the girls' state basketball tournament in Virginia in '52, and that was important to her, so I always looked up to her for going into a pretty much male-dominated field." When Teresa's mother first approached basketball officials about becoming a referee, they looked at her and said, "'Lady, you've got five kids. Why do you want to come back and ref?' And she said, 'Because I love the game and I want to do it,' and they said, 'Well, you have to take the test.' And she said, 'Well, give me the test,' and she passed, so they started giving her refing assignments. I thought that was very interesting that she was one of the first female refs in the state."

Aunt Alberta, meanwhile, the first blond to enter the family, has been christened the Rose Kennedy of the Isaacs. "Aunt Alberta has always been politically involved. We always called her Rose Kennedy Alberta Isaac, 'cause she . . . was always very, very politically active in the Democratic Women's Club, and she kind of made sure all of us got involved. You wouldn't find an event in town that she wasn't at. She was very active in [Governor] Beshear's first campaign for state representative and attorney general, very active in his campaigns. She was a real powerhouse on the north side of town. If you wanted to run for anything, you went and talked to her, 'cause she had that extended family connection. She could work our network and get you up and running with a bunch of yard signs just through our family."

Most poignantly, Teresa turns to the story of her mother's grandmother, her great-grandmother from Lebanon. "She was fourteen and she went down to the boat dock and jumped on a boat. . . . She had no idea where she was going. She just stowed away on a boat. My mother's told me that story since I was a little girl." These are the stories that Teresa wants to impart to the younger generation. "Whenever we see anyone that's interested, we try to cultivate that [fearlessness] in them and say, 'Yeah, you can do it too.' So we're trying to encourage that fearlessness in the next generation of girls in the family."

Teresa has demonstrated her own fearlessness to the younger generation. When traveling in Pakistan for the State Department, for instance,

Teresa could not deny that fear was part of her repertoire of emotions. "Everybody had to walk through a metal detector, and they have bomb-sniffing dogs, and I had an escort. There were Pakistani police in front of me and Pakistani police behind me, and then a machine gun in the car with me, and I traveled in an armored vehicle. It was tense in Pakistan. Yeah, Pakistan was a little scary, especially now when I see what happened in Lahore. The whole time I was there, they took the U.S. embassy license plate off of the vehicle I was in, and they kept it in the front seat, and when there were guards, they would hold it up to them and show it to them, but they were afraid that it would be a target if it was on the back [of the car]."

Rather than dwelling on such fearful encounters, Teresa, sounding like a politician, pulls back from her individual experiences to focus on the role women can play generally. "I think that women need to have a very strong policy-making role. I think women are much better at trying to build consensus and bring people together, and I think women care more about the future of children, so I think they have a greater passion about making the world a better place for children." The women in Uganda, for instance, "are very passionate about the same kinds of things that we care about here. They want a better life for their children. They want better schools. They want better infrastructure. They want better domestic violence prosecution. They want to help women start their own businesses, so you can relate very easily to what they're interested in, and you can show them steps for how to do whatever it is they want to do. You or I can relate instantly to them, and once they realize there will be a lot of give-and-take, then they participate. . . . They would tell me stories of things that had happened in their area and what they hoped to improve, and I would just tell them what strategies [to use and] how to deal [with their problems]. Then they would sing their songs for me and do their dances for me. It was very sweet. The State Department people said, 'That means they're happy and like what you told them, because when they do this particular dance, it's their happy dance.' It was very nice."

ALIGNING EXCEPTIONAL ARABS AND JEWS

What does Teresa have in common with Sarah and Frances? These three women, along with their families, share much despite their religious, ethnic, and generational differences. Parallel lives unfolded in opposite parts of the state. One family in rural eastern Kentucky and another in small-town western Kentucky accomplished similar feats during the same period. They made it financially and socially as outsiders, and they did so publicly. They were proud, prominent, and sophisticated. Theirs is the story of the American dream.

What is conspicuous is that both families tended toward the dramatic. Joe Junior described his father as a showman. Howard depicted his aunt Sarah as an artist and her store as a blank canvas. These fine men and women were like actors on a stage, presenting themselves to their communities (or, as in the case of Alene, actually taking the stage). They engineered business productions to be consumed by the whole community, whether performances at one of the Isaacs' theaters or Sarah's radio or fashion shows. Their well-thought-out attire made them stand out and be noticed in rural Kentucky. Mr. Isaac, with his imported hat and suit, approached the community with dignity. Sarah did the same in Hopkinsville, as exemplified by her ability to leave problems behind in the back room and walk onto the sales floor with aplomb. The beauty of Alene and her sisters stood out in small-town Kentucky. And both families turned to New York to make their dramatic effects more remarkable—their theaters more glorious, and their stores more urbane. As good actors, they negotiated multiple stages, connecting with their respective communities in Kentucky, their contacts in New York, and their assorted public and private acquaintances. For the Myers sisters, Frances in particular, negotiating these multiple stages could be a strain. Teresa used her family's acting agility to take the political stage locally, nationally, and internationally. It may well be that isolated Arabs or Jews aspire to achieve beyond local expectations, proving themselves at once part of the local community and beyond it as well.

Both these families were politically active Democrats. Although Sarah and Frances didn't publicize their political leanings, they were strong Democrats, as witnessed by their attendance at President Carter's inauguration. The Isaacs, likewise, are staunch Democrats.[6] Politics can even bring Arabs and Jews together in Kentucky. One of the first things Joe Junior said to me when I came to chat with him and Alberta was, "Your aunt worked on my daughter's campaign to be a judge."

Today, both Teresa Isaac and Howard Myers, who are about the same age (mid-fifties to early sixties), are interested in bridging the gaps between Arabs and Jews. Their political inclinations matter. They act on their political beliefs—Teresa as an international educator, and Howard as a board member of the Central Kentucky Council for Peace and Justice. They have crossed paths in their respective political work and now articulate the dramatic inclinations of earlier generations in the political arena rather than in the family businesses.

Finally, all three women, despite their generational, regional, and ethnic differences, have demonstrated a commitment to other women, and they crossed boundaries in doing so. Sarah and Frances defied the gender ideals of their day that relegated white middle-class women to the home to focus on domestic chores. Under the guise of creating the idealized and traditional woman in their store, the never-married Myers sisters led decidedly nonstandard lives, yet they devoted themselves to both the standard and the nonstandard woman. It's rousing to hear Howard quote his aunt Sarah's motto: "I want every woman that walks into this store to feel like they're the most important woman in the world, and I want them to feel like they have the absolutely best dress." Yet they also challenged traditional gender roles through their Sunday poolside cocktail parties, business drive, and mentoring practices. Today, Teresa openly stresses the need for female politicians, even though their presence is no longer extraordinary. But it is important to keep in mind that Teresa is no ordinary female politician: she is a publicly self-identifying Arab American former mayor of a midsized, Middle American city with Appalachian roots. She is not the norm, but the exception, and her identity, with its multiple facets, enables her to crisscross many boundaries.

Sarah and Frances Myers and Teresa Isaac were and are exceptional women, and Kentucky offered them the opportunity to express their talents publicly.

3

Maternal Echoes

Expectations are high for mothers. Women are supposed to mother, and they are supposed to do it well. That's a lot of pressure. Some almost mythic renderings assume that women come into their own in the company of children and that good mothers relinquish any sense of self with the advent of offspring. As unrealistic (or outdated) as these expectations may sound, idealized notions of mothers are remarkably resistant to change.

Perceptions of ethnic mothers, particularly from the past, suppose that these child protectors cater to their children's every need without question.[1] They are hypermothers who lavish excessive attention on their children and are always ready with an arsenal of chicken noodle soup and other nurturing tonics should the need arise. These hovering mothers, with hawk-like vision, are able to discern whether the people around their children will diminish or enrich their offspring's present and future lives. These maternal stereotypes, however, do not always reflect reality, especially when mothers work outside of the home.

Gishie Bloomfield and Elsie Nasief were born and raised in Kentucky's largest cities—Lexington and Louisville, respectively—and went about their lives like many Jews and Arabs in their communities, without drama or dramatic expectations. Their family businesses were not elaborate creations that later generations glamorized but rather modest enterprises intended to establish the families financially. Despite their differences, Elsie and Gishie resemble Sarah and Frances Myers and Teresa Isaac, in that they did not adhere to popular conceptions about mothering.

Gishie Bloomfield married and raised three daughters. Yet motherhood did not interfere with her outside interests, such as the store she ran with her husband, her investments, her rental property, and her community activities. According to her daughter, Simone Salomon, Gishie simply went about her life with little thought that she might not be meeting maternal benchmarks, even though standards are high for Jewish mothers. Elsie Nasief, meanwhile, neither married nor had children in an era (the 1940s and 1950s) when most Lebanese girls did so. Yet maternity has enveloped her. Although Elsie is in her eighties and her mother has been dead for maybe fifty years, her Lebanese mother's presence is obvious when Elsie recounts her own story. Elsie's multiple visits to Lebanon and her continued association with the Orthodox church in Louisville venerate her mother. Today, Elsie, as the oldest member of her family, is a link to the past for her numerous nieces and nephews and their offspring, to whom being Lebanese may be nothing more than a food memory. Despite having no children of her own, Elsie has assumed a maternal role.

In this chapter, the Arab mothering nonmother is placed alongside the Jewish nonmothering mother. Their stories are the inverse of each other. The Jewish woman married and had children but, as a feminist, was preoccupied with other concerns. The Arab woman never married or had children but gladly assumed a maternal role, learning the art from her own mother.

Their stories are not just singular; they transcend generations. Thus, their maternal tales are conveyed relationally between mothers and daughters. Daughters sometimes perceive their relationships with their mothers to be almost spiritual, transcending even death. I recall that when a friend's grandmother died, her Italian mother commented that the grandmother had left her own body and entered the mother's.[2] This image comes to mind when I think of Gishie Bloomfield and Elsie Nasief and the mothers and daughters surrounding them.

GISHIE BLOOMFIELD
THE NEW WAY SHOE SHOP
LEXINGTON, KENTUCKY

"You know how you always wish for what you didn't have?" asked Simone Salomon, laughing. "I think our friends thought it was pretty neat because we were on our own, and we didn't have a lot of rules or anything, but at least *I* did want a more typical mom." Simone tells her mother's story with honesty, acceptance, love, perspective, and even humor. Her mother didn't focus on her children and wasn't the ideal mother that Simone once desired, but she can laugh about it now and admire her mother's ways. "Even though, when I was little, she wasn't like the other Jewish moms . . . who were so nurturing, now I really admire her." Perhaps it has taken the passage of time or even her mother's death for Simone to gain perspective and levity. Her mother, Gishie Bloomfield, died in 1995 at age seventy-three. Of course, even after a mother dies, anger can linger because she didn't live up to expectations or wasn't adept at what mothers are supposed to do—namely, nurture. Simone, who is now in her sixties and the mother of grown children, understands that resenting Gishie isn't a worthwhile pastime. "What can you do? I think you're a certain age; you're an adult, you just have to get over things. You can't want something from Mom that Mom couldn't ever give." Gishie Bloomfield was many things: a dedicated saleswoman, a Jew without any particular attachment to the religion, an advocate for social justice, and, of course, a mother. I tell Gishie's maternal story in relation to her daughter, Simone, who narrates her mother's tale; in relation to the community where she resided; and in relation to her husband, Julian, and her mother, Sadie Bederman (or, as Simone and her sisters called their grandmother, "Bube").

Simone has consciously oriented her own life differently from her mother's, and she grasps that she has enjoyed her life more than her mother ever could. "Mom would never go out with a girlfriend like I do and drink with her girlfriends. I don't think I'm quite as type A and impatient as she was. I was a real mother. I really enjoyed my children; that was my job. I don't think she particularly loved having children. I think I was much more traditional as far as how I raised my kids. I think I realized that I wished that she had been there more after school like I always was."

Simone exudes elegance, sophistication, and self-confidence. She is draped in lovely clothes, and although she still resides in her hometown of Lexington, she is familiar with New York and other urban locales. Her present looks and demeanor hide the fact that, as a child, she was shy, as were her two younger sisters. "I always felt like I was different," Simone admitted. "We did have some friends, and then there were other people

Simone Salomon. (Photo by Sarah Jane Sanders.)

that were Jewish that were a lot more integrated into school than we were. We were shy, so I don't know if it had as much to do with being Jewish as just being shy. We lived on Versailles Road, and there were no kids there, so the three of us stuck together. When we were young, it was just the three of us." They found some refuge among other Jewish kids. "We went to Friday night services, but we weren't Shabbat observant. We liked to go. The kids all sat up front. We sat up front, and we'd see all our friends. It wasn't like it is now, where parents entertain their kids and they're running around. We were bored, so it was a good thing to do."

Their identities were first and foremost Jewish. In the Lexington that Simone grew up in, Jews from the Conservative synagogue mostly kept to themselves. "They [Gishie's family] weren't religious at all. They were Russian communists. They were very secular." But even so, Gishie's family associated with the synagogue in town. "They belonged to the synagogue, and she [Gishie] was in the youth group and her friends were Jewish. All her friends that I knew were Jewish." Jews from the synagogue worked with one another and socialized with their own. While the larger non-Jewish community attended church on Sunday mornings, Jews congregated at Mr. Goller's kosher butcher shop for corned beef sandwiches and an earful from the proprietor.[3] It's hard to imagine, but in the 1940s and 1950s, Jews from the synagogue in Lexington lived in such close proximity to one another that Christians retreated into the background.[4]

Gishie's family, like the other Jews in their community, possessed decidedly Jewish immigrant tales. Gishie, for example, was born in 1921 in Lexington to Lithuanian Jewish immigrants who came from the same *shtetl*, Pushelot (also spelled Pushelat), as many of the other Jews in the area. Any knowledge about Lithuania that Simone and her sisters possessed came through Gishie's Lithuanian mother, their grandmother, Bube (Yiddish for "grandmother"). Bube guaranteed that her granddaughters knew about her heartache in Lithuania. "My grandmother had stories," said Simone. "She was nineteen before she left [Lithuania]. She had a boyfriend and he came over, and I guess great-grandfather didn't like him and threw him out of the house through the window, and she left without him. Of course, [she] never saw him again." Simone asked her sister, Janice, "Did you ever hear that story? And Janice replied, "I sure did—every day." Although Bube mourned her lost love in the old country,

Gishie and Julian Bloomfield. (Courtesy Simone Salomon.)

she otherwise considered Europe unworthy of attention, even if, in Simone's estimation, Bube herself was still very much of the old country, with her Yiddish witticisms, Yiddish sayings, and Yiddish practices.

As a single woman, Gishie's orbit consisted of other Jews, her mother, and her work. That orbit became even smaller with her marriage to Julian in 1942, on the same day she graduated from the University of Kentucky. Afterward, one gets the sense from Simone that Gishie and Julian barely looked beyond each other. "They did everything together. They had an incredible marriage. They were always making out and smooching, and [calling each other] honey and sweetie. They liked being together all the time. Neither one of them did anything without the other one. They didn't have any hobbies. They didn't belong to anything. It was just the two of them." Simone's narration of her mother's story, not surprisingly, often blends her mother's and father's lives, as though they were one; this was most noticeable in their dedication to the store. Yet despite their close marriage, Gishie never knew about her husband's earlier life in Germany.

Julian fled Germany in 1936 at age twenty-six, after his father was murdered by the Nazis. The death was a tightly guarded secret because Julian and his family had been told that his father had committed suicide. Julian immigrated to Kentucky, joining an uncle and a brother who were already there. His start in Kentucky was humble, working for Jewish store owners and living in a communal arrangement. "His first job was at Meyers cutting riding hats," Simone said. "He made five dollars a week and ate an apple every day for lunch. He also lived in a boarding kind of house. . . . Actually, he was sharing the bed [with another boarder, but] he didn't know it because he couldn't speak enough English. . . . He thought it was just his room."

Notwithstanding his modest accommodations in Kentucky, Julian was committed to this country and tried to forget about Germany, even though the memories haunted him. "When he left Germany, that was the end of it. And in fact, he would not even speak German to people who came into the store. One time he said he tried to help somebody who couldn't speak English and they said, 'Oh, you speak nice German. Where did you learn?' And he said at school. He also had trouble remembering. His mother told him not to tell anyone [about his father's death], and he never even told my mother," Simone said. "So he kept that in, and he kept having nightmares."

Privately and publicly, Julian relinquished all things German. He made it clear that the past was not to be dusted off by Gishie or the girls. "We [Simone and her sisters] were afraid to ask. It was just something you knew you didn't talk about. She [Gishie] never talked about it, and then I found out later when we took Dad back to Germany that there were things that he never even told my mother, in sixty-five years, never told anyone." The past and its difficulties were shelved, even if the silence protecting the past was apparent.

Julian respected his mother's wishes, refusing to utter a word about the circumstances surrounding his father's death even to Gishie, his clos-est companion, and Gishie lived with the consequences of his decision to adhere to his mother's orders. Gishie was not one to dwell on past or pres-ent difficulties in an emotional way, however. Rather, Gishie, alongside Julian, focused on things of more pragmatic import—namely, the store.

The family business, the New Way Shoe Shop, was run by Gishie's par-ents. During World War II, just after Julian became a U.S. citizen, he was drafted into the army. "As soon as he became a citizen, they drafted him, and he was gone for four years," Simone said. Gishie followed him to mili-tary bases in the United States and even participated in the war effort her-self. "She was a Rosie the Riveter when he was in California. She was proud of being one. . . . When he got shipped overseas, that's when she came home." While Julian was deployed overseas, Gishie's father died unexpect-edly, and Gishie had to become a shopkeeper. "Her father died, so she ran the shoe store. She really took responsibility for the store. Her sisters didn't live in Lexington." At least temporarily, the store was run solely by women. "Bube worked in the store at least until my father came back from the war," said Simone. "When Dad came back, that's when Bube didn't come down anymore, and they [Gishie and Julian] went into business together."

The shoe and shoe repair shop provided for Gishie's family. "I think that they [Simone's grandparents] were pretty well off, and they had a house which, at the time, I think, was considered a really nice house. I never knew my grandfather; he died before I was born. But they said he liked to have the finest of everything and even had custom-made shirts with his initials on them. He had a nice car and only drove it on Sun-days." The life Gishie built with Julian centered on this store, which had endowed Gishie's family with some financial stability. But nothing about the store appealed to Simone. "I never cared for retail business. I never wanted to go to the store. I never wanted anything to do with the store. It wasn't my thing. I think maybe I resented it [because] they were gone there all day, and when they'd come home, they'd talk about it."

Starting around 1919, the business was located in downtown Lexing-ton. It eventually moved from one building to another, and in both places the layouts required Gishie and Julian to work physically. "It [the original store] was kind of a long space," Simone recalled, with merchandise "on either side, floor to ceiling. They ended up going up and down the ladders [a lot]. And then there were showcases. It was pretty crowded. There was a lot of stuff in there. When they moved next door, there was like a two-story building. They had a landing, where they had the office, and they'd go to the second floor, and they had merchandise up there, and there was a basement where they had merchandise stored, so they were up and down three flights of stairs all day long." Possibly least appealing to Simone was the shoe repairman her parents hired. "It was hard to find a shoe repairman that was reliable. We were always scared of them. Dad was always bailing them out of jail. We were always scared that the shoe repairman was going to kill Dad. He tried to kill his wife, slit her throat, and Dad bailed him out. So, yeah, we'd hear them [Gishie and Julian] talking about them. They weren't the most refined people in the world, so we'd hear these stories, and I was always scared."

Simone found much about the store displeasing, but Gishie and Julian were consumed with stocking merchandise to meet the varied and fickle tastes of their customers. "It started out being more shoes, and it was . . . men's shoes. At that time, they still had the shoe repair in the back, and over time, it became more boots and riding apparel, western boots. So they had anybody in there from farmers to horse people. Then they went through periods where Davy Crockett and all that was popular—the coonskin hats. The young kids would come in there and get their cowboy boots for Christmas and their hats. Then later on, they started carrying Italian shoes, so they had a big black clientele too. So there was a wide variety of people in there."

From Simone's perspective, the store was what mattered most to Gishie and Julian. "They were gone there all day," she said, "and then they'd come home, they'd talk about it. They'd talk about the store, the customers, the nice ones, and the ones that weren't so nice. They'd rehash their whole day. They worked together all day and then they'd come home and talk about the customers and the store. It wasn't like they asked us [the three girls] about what happened at school or anything. . . . They were very much into one another." Outside distractions did not exist for Gishie and Julian. Vacations were not a possibility. "For years, there was never any vacation. We never took a vacation ever. They did not feel that they could ever leave the store or leave it with anybody. They didn't trust anyone, and I guess they would have said that they really couldn't afford to hire somebody else. In the early years, they didn't have any employees at all. It was just the two of them, and one of them would go over to the drugstore and sit on the stool and just watch the store. They didn't have any help, and they never took vacations." The store resided in the family like a treasured member.

With Gishie and Julian fixated on their cherished store, where were their three daughters? A series of hired helpers tended to the girls at home. "We had a man for a while. I don't know where they found him, and he was always smoking and his fingers were always really yellow; he had white hair. And then just a whole series of maids, nothing long term." One maid relied on the girls to do her work. "We had one maid. I'll never forget. She was a big, big lady, and she'd take the bus, and by the time she got to our house, she was exhausted, so we'd all clean the house, my sisters and I would clean for her." Eventually, Simone, the eldest child, assumed responsibility for the household, and the maids disappeared. "By the time I was ten or eleven, I was kind of looking after my sisters, and we'd come home from school and we'd be by ourselves." Sickness was out of the question. Simone recalled that she and her sisters were "never sick; we never stayed home from school ever." Simone took on cooking responsibilities too. "She [Gishie] wasn't a wonderful cook, and actually I started to cook at a pretty young age because I love to cook. She might have made something ahead of time, and I'd warm it up and make a salad, but when they came home from the store, I'd have dinner."

Carved into Simone's memory are summers spent at the Carnahan House, a country club of sorts. Their mother would drop them off in the morning and then dash to the store. "In the summer, Mother would take us out to Carnahan House. It was on Newtown Pike and it was the University Club. And Mom would leave us out there before work, and the three of us would stay out there all day; then she'd pick us up. [It] was not a terrible place—because it had a pool and tennis courts and a place to eat—unless it was a rainy day and we were the only three kids out there in the rain [laughing]. . . . There was a clubhouse, and we could go in there and just hang around, play pool or Ping-Pong, and they had a little dollhouse outside [where] we could play house, entertain ourselves. In Mom's eyes, she was taking us to a country club and . . . thought we were very lucky to be doing this."

On Saturdays—a busy workday for their parents—the girls roamed the lively and busy downtown area. "There was not a lot of time for us, and they worked on Saturday too. Saturday was their big day at the store. We had no curfews, nothing. We'd take the bus downtown on Saturdays and go to movies and go to eat." The downtown Lexington that Simone and her sisters encountered in the 1950s and 1960s was a Jewish one. "All the stores were downtown. Most of the stores that I can remember were all Jewish, like Baker's, where we used to get our shoes. Pretty much we are talking Main Street: Lowenthal's, Wolf Wiles, Bloomfield's. When they closed for the [Jewish High] Holidays, I don't think there was much open." Simone and her sisters found enjoyment, comfort, and connection with the Jews surrounding them in downtown Lexington.

Ensconced in a deep partnership that revolved around each other and the store, Gishie and Julian kept outside interferences at bay. They didn't spend much time chatting with the other Jewish merchants downtown. Whereas other shop owners might go out to lunch, Simone's parents brought their lunch with them. "Mom would stop at my grandmother's every morning, and my grandmother made lunch. She'd stop there and pick up lunch." As far as socializing, "maybe they played cards with other Jews, but just Jews from the synagogue. They weren't very social, and it wouldn't be anybody from the temple. Their friends were all synagogue people."

Simone noticed that other Jewish mothers were not as busy as her own, particularly after the Bloomfields moved to a neighborhood with plenty of other Jewish families. "The Lowenthals were there, us, the Levys, the Steins, the Waldmans, the Sterns, and the Jacobs—on one block, there were seven Jewish families. I lived in the Steins' house. The best thing to me would be to go up the street to the Steins, and Anne [Mrs. Stein] would sit and talk to you for hours, and I just thought that was so neat, because if Mom was home, she was busy vacuuming. She never sat down. You'd see her sit down you'd think she was sick, which she never was."

Landmark events took a backseat because of her parents' devotion to the store, and Gishie never doubted her choices. Simone recalled, "They still wouldn't leave the store even when I got married. The day I got married, they worked; they didn't close the store. They stayed down there all day, and we had company from out of town." Although they didn't miss the wedding itself, they didn't participate in the preparations, such as set-ting up the chuppah (the wedding canopy). Later, according to Simone, Gishie didn't ask herself, "'What was I thinking? What was I doing?' It just never occurred to her not to go to the store."

Despite Simone's hope to the contrary, Gishie didn't embrace being a grandmother, and feelings of abandonment surface when Simone dis-cusses her parents' retirement to Florida in the early 1980s. "No, that was another sore spot. [There was no] help raising the kids, even when they [Gishie and Julian] were here. Mom was not that involved, [but] they baby-sat a few times." Julian was a more hands-on grandfather to Simone's boys. "He'd come two mornings a week before they went to school, when they were little, and brought them breakfast from McDonald's—brought them a Happy Meal and sat with them—so they'll always remember that about Grandpa. But Mom, never. When they left I was thirty-six years old, and I felt like an orphan. I felt like I had been abandoned, but I don't think I should have expected anything else. . . . I'm pretty independent."

Now, Simone sees the humor in her mother's actions. In Florida, Gishie avoided spending time with her grandchildren when they visited from Kentucky. "When she had a chance as a grandmother, . . . instead of playing with them, she'd be on the phone all day talking with her stock-broker [*laughing*]. . . . You'd think . . . she'd plan the time out to do things with them. But I don't think she really regretted that she wasn't with us [her daughters], so she was going to do [the same thing] with the [grand] kids."

Julian was less preoccupied than Gishie with accumulating wealth, and he also had an appreciation for aesthetics. "She was a lot more wor-ried about money and what they had," said Simone. "She was working full-time, and she was actually much more interested in business and investments and stuff than Dad. He'd let Mom take care of that part. He was more into flowers and stuff. He liked aesthetics. He liked gardening. He ironed his own shirts. He was the only one in the family that could iron. Mom or none of us [girls] could iron. He was very neat, very neat. It's funny, because even in later years, she would buy stock; she was the one that really worried about all that. The story is that she woke up Dad one night and said, 'Do you have any idea what we're worth?' And he said, 'No' and went back to sleep. And she would dwell on all that. He was just happy to go to work and run the business and let her take care of everything else." Everything else included the rental properties Gishie decided the family needed. "Well, I think Dad paid the bills, but she was always figuring things out and what they should invest in. She also went and started buying properties and renting things out, and it was always a hassle because people were always messing things up or something didn't work. She was always having to clean up. It was pretty horrible, but she was concerned about accumulating money."

Gishie's natural drive also emerged on the sales floor with her determined and unidirectional sales strategy. "She was like a really hard sell. If she didn't have what they [the customers] were looking for, she'd drag everything else out and show them everything. It was hard to get away from her. She was a saleswoman. Her idea was not to let them out of the store without [buying] something."

Of course, Gishie, unlike her husband, also had domestic obligations. She arrived at work later than her husband did because she would take the girls to school or to the country club in the morning. "Dad would go down there really early in the morning. I think he'd be down there at seven o'clock, and Mom probably didn't come till nine or so." Gishie was also obliged to help her own mother. "She usually took one day a week off from the store, but on that day she'd take my grandmother, who didn't drive, to the grocery. . . . She was always at the store or helping our grandmother [Bube]."

Bube was an important figure in their lives. All Jewish holidays and Sundays were spent at Bube's house. "She was a big part of our lives. We spent a lot of time with her. In addition to eating over there all the time, we'd go there every Sunday after Sunday school for lunch, and those were the days when nothing was open [on Sunday], so we'd sit on the front porch and she'd make homemade lemonade. There was nothing to do, basically." Bube regularly fed her granddaughters, even if her cooking wasn't great. "She wasn't a wonderful cook either, but she cooked a lot for us."

Bube's ways were often comical and reminiscent of another land. She was strong but loving. "She worked hard her whole life. She worked in the store at least until my father came back from the war, and then she and her second husband had a little store on Broadway. It was a little clothing store. It was called the Family Circle, and she worked there, but I don't think she really loved it. By the time my sisters and me [came along], we were her life." Bube was full of contradictions; she was both tough and fearful. "She was a businesswoman. She was brutal, but she was very generous with us and with people who needed something. Somebody tried to steal her groceries once, and she chased them. [But] she didn't drive. She tried once and was scared."

Bube had strong convictions: no doctors, no banks, and no long conversations on the telephone. "[She] didn't believe in banks, didn't believe in doctors. She was a real Russian old-fashioned lady. My grandmother had the idea that you could cure anything with hot water and Vick's salve. And she didn't believe in banking either. She liked to keep her money where she could get to it, in the back of picture frames." That's where Simone got the money to buy her first car. "So this is really funny," she said. "When I went to buy my first car, I went to Bube to borrow the money. My parents were in Israel, but they had convinced her to take some of the money in the house and put it in the bank, so she was all upset because she wasn't sure if she still had enough cash in the house to buy my car. She was going all around, and she counted the whole thing out. . . . I paid her back every month until it was paid. . . . I think it was $800, $1,000. Then she had this little jar in the pantry, and every time I paid her back, she'd just put it in the jar, and when I paid her all back, she gave me the whole jar." Bube distrusted institutions and technology, including the telephone. When Bube's daughter (Gishie's sister) called from her honeymoon, "Bube hung up on her. She didn't want to talk on the phone."

Bube dwelled in the Jewish world of Lexington, even if she wasn't religious. "I don't think Bube ever stepped foot in the synagogue. If my sisters and I were in a play, she might come, but not for services." Yet Bube's frame of reference rested with other Jewish women. "She spoke Yiddish, and she had a whole bunch of friends in town, like Mrs. Godhelf and Mrs. Rosenman. They all called each other by their married names, even though they were best friends; it was like, 'Ms. Moosnick, how nice to see you.' They were very formal. None of them drove. I think they'd wait until the men took them, and then they'd get together and play cards and go to each other's houses." Yiddish humor and sensibilities imbued Bube. "You'd say, 'How are you, Bube?'" And she'd reply, "'Oh, I'm so happy I could lie down and die.'"

Gishie and her mother "were really close. They talked and saw each other every day," said Simone. And they had similar ways. As noted earlier, cooking was not their forte, but Bube was an inventive cook. "One of the things she used to make, she'd make these chicken hamburgers, and we used to laugh at her. She'd grind the chicken, but she was way ahead of her time because now they're doing chicken burgers." Being affectionate was not one of their character traits either. "She [Bube] was nurturing with her grandchildren. I'm not sure how she was with her children as far as being affectionate. I'm not sure that any of them were touchy-feely." Strength and conviction permeated their styles. "They were both really strong women, stubborn. They both hated doctors, didn't believe in doctors. They felt hot water could take care of anything. Best to stay away from doctors." Religion bored them, yet being Jewish epitomized them. "Culturally, they were Jewish." Yiddish was the language of choice between this mother and daughter; they shared a level of intimacy through a language that escaped others. "To Bube, Mom spoke Yiddish, but I never heard her speak Yiddish to anybody else." They spoke Yiddish "when they didn't want us to know what they were talking about." Current events and the news consumed them. "She [Bube] dwelled on the news, and whatever was happening in the news was breaking her heart. She talked a lot about the news and she was so upset, kids dying. She always took it very personally. They both were slightly depressive." As is often the case, features of our mothers become our own, and Gishie was no different in this regard.

Not surprisingly, just as Simone can laugh and giggle about Bube, there are things about her mother that she finds amusing and admirable. Gishie had a rebellious streak, similar to her mother's, and rejected things religious. "Mom was not religious at all. She was very bored by [it]. She'd go [to synagogue] on the holidays and . . . her eyes [would be] rolling in the back of her head. She'd get out her lipstick and put it on while she was sitting there, not too interested. She was so put out [and thought] that it was a waste of time. She'd rather be vacuuming or something. Dad was always religious. He'd go to services. He'd daven every morning. It didn't seem to affect their relationship any [*laughing*]. It was kind of live and let live." Julian probably would have liked a kosher home, but Gishie didn't comply. "My dad was kosher when he grew up, . . . but my mom was so on the opposite end of the spectrum. They ate everything. I don't think she even knew anything about kosher. I don't think she knew about meat and dairy mixing and all that." Gishie loathed that kind of religious protocol and made her thoughts known.

Gishie even rebelled against expectations that she would participate in synagogue activities like the other women in the community did. Yet, this is not to say that she wasn't interested in Judaism. According to Simone, Gishie was charitable and gave to Jewish efforts that spoke to her. "They gave to everything and not for themselves. We didn't have a lot, and they didn't have a lot of things. My mother didn't own any jewelry. They didn't care about that, but they would give to any charity that asked. Her favorite thing was Boys' Town in Jerusalem. She really liked that because they were in Israel, and she just fell in love. And I think it was because she didn't have any boys that she liked the Boys' Town. She called them 'her boys.'"

Gishie did her own thing, and much to my surprise, that included enjoying a good cocktail. "No, she actually did [drink] and smoked too," said Simone. "When they went out or there was something at the synagogue, she could get a little tipsy, and I think she liked it. And then when they moved to Florida, I think they started having more cocktails in the afternoon with friends."

Other quirky things about her mother can make Simone chuckle. "She was pretty strong physically, actually. She was a PE [physical education] major in school. And she took judo lessons. I forgot [*laughing*]. She was going to protect herself." Gishie's intense resolve could make her singularly aware of the task at hand and unaware of those around her, such as other drivers on the road. "She was a crazy driver, too. Oh, she was really fast. She was always in a hurry, and one day we were coming down Broadway, and someone opened their door on the street side and she just took the door off." One's impression is that Gishie was a tenacious woman who cared little about others' interpretations of her actions. She didn't self-evaluate or self-reflect, and she never questioned or doubted her maternal actions or inactions—an anomaly in our age of self- and even hyperreflection. "I don't know that Mom was very introspective. I don't think she thought a lot about herself," Simone observed. Rather, she went about her life with little concern for how others regarded her.

Gishie took her ability to focus and applied it not only to business concerns but also to political matters. Simone's pride in her mother's political doggedness is obvious. "She was definitely a feminist—big for the underdog. On the way downtown, she would see a black person on the street waiting for the bus, [and] she'd pick them up and take them. She'd sit in the back of the bus with the black people. . . . We always had to do everything to help stand up for people. She was political." Gishie did not keep her political views to herself; she voiced them in the local newspaper as a frequent writer of letters to the editor. "She was a voracious letter writer to the paper. Oh my gosh, she [wrote some] gorgeous letters, I mean, unbelievable. Every injustice, everything that made her mad, she would write." Simone described her mother's last letter to the editor before she died: "It was about hate, because evidently she had written something (and I don't know what she had written on), but somebody had written back and . . . had picked up by her name that she was Jewish. It was kind of a hate-filled thing. So she wrote in answer to this person about hate and prejudice and [said that] the thing she was proudest of was that her children never hated anybody different from them for any reason." In the letter, Gishie's maternal pride was effusive.

Through the years I have written many letters to the Editor that I was happy to been deemed worthy of appearing in your paper. My "fan mail" and telephone calls both in agreement and disagreement has been interesting. The beauty of the political process in this Country is that everyone has a right to express their opinion. I was saddened to have received a crude, unsigned note after my last letter appeared. The person knew nothing about me, and did not bother to reject my opinions. Obviously, the person was displeased only by my name and the religion the person assumed was indicated by the name.
  I have been married for 52 years, and in the four generations since my parents came to this Country, no member of my family has ever been in jail, received welfare, or failed to help others because of their religion, race, or ethnicity. We have taken our responsibility as citizens seriously; informing ourselves, expressing opinions, becoming involved in the

political process, writing letters to our Representatives in Congress, and always voting. My name will never appear in "Who's Who in America," but I feel my greatest contributions to this Country are my three children who do not know the meaning of hate or bigotry. To my knowledge, my children and grandchildren have never in their actions or hearts espoused unthinking hatred toward another human being. When necessary, they have taken public stands to back up their beliefs in the equality of all people.

If I could change one thing, it would be the senseless hatred handed down from generation to generation that is tearing our Country apart. By failing to use our diversity as a strength, we will all be weakened. Isn't it time, as Barbara Jordan said years ago, to start making the reality of this Country fit the creed of this Country?

Gishie Bloomfield

December 1994

Gishie's political activities brought successes that can still be seen today. Gishie and Julian fought development in their neighborhood, and it was a battle they won. Today, their former neighborhood lacks unseemly structures and boasts only buildings that fit the residential landscape. "We lived on Idle Hour Drive, and they left those two lots that face Richmond Road there for development. [My parents] didn't want anything commercial there like a gas station, and they'd fight. They spent a lot of time and a lot of money on the neighborhood. Finally, [developers] were going to put in a bank, and [my parents] didn't even want the bank; they didn't want anything. They fought years and years, until now [we have] those beautiful apartments, so it worked. They kept anything bad from going up there."

Simone savors the political ideas and impulses to action that her mother passed down to her. "We're all big Democrats, and they were Democrats. They also had a lot of zoning issues on the street, so it was good for us to see a grassroots thing. There was always something going on in the neighborhood, with them having meetings and protesting this and having signs and going down to the council. That was the way I grew up; that was a huge part of our family. Yeah, a lot of my ideas come from [my mother], definitely." In Simone's estimation, the best family times revolved around politics. "Well, first of all, [my family was] on top of the news all the time, interested in politics—local, national, and world—always talking about politics. And my best times that I can remember as a family were watching the returns, conventions, speeches. We were all glued to it, and . . . we're all like that. I was very sad that my mom wasn't here to see [Obama's] election, 'cause it would have been really wonderful for her."

Simone appreciates her mother's political activities and enthusiasm; she also grasps the cultural climate her mother confronted as a woman. Gishie graduated from the University of Kentucky in 1942, at a time when women didn't regularly attend college. "She went to the University of Kentucky. Her sisters did too, which at that time was really unusual. They all went to college. Her sister was the first female editor of the *Kentucky Kernel* [the school paper]. Mom was a PE teacher really. She got her degree and she did some physical therapy on the side. Mom said a couple of times, maybe there were other things she could have done 'cause she was a college graduate. So if she didn't have to be in the store, there were other things she could do, but she felt she had to be in the store." And Simone recognizes that maybe her mother mothered because that is what a woman was supposed to do, not because she had an express desire to have children. "I don't think she particularly loved having children. I think that was the thing you did. I think so. Well, she was not a very maternal person. She was much more interested in business, politics, being involved in things. I was thinking about this. I never heard her say, 'I wish I didn't have to work; I'd rather be home with you all.' I don't think that was the case. She did say once [that] when we were little was a happy time for her."

In our day-to-day lives, mothers who are no longer with us surface—a piece of food, a word, or a smell can stir memories. As Simone simply said, "I think about her a lot." And of late, Simone avoids dwelling on what her mother wasn't and focuses on what she was. Gishie's eccentricities stand out, including her diet, which consisted of chocolate and diet Coke, and her habit of ordering the cheapest dish on a menu and then complaining about the quality of the food.

ELSIE NASIEF
NASIEF BROTHERS
LOUISVILLE, KENTUCKY

"My oldest brother married, but he didn't have any children. My other brother and I didn't marry, and I guess I was too busy working." This short statement says a lot about Elsie Nasief, who is in her eighties. It offers a glimpse into Elsie's early work life at the family meat-processing plant and grocery store, to which she devotes relatively little attention in telling her story. Nor does she dwell on the fact that she never had children, because Elsie's maternal love for her nieces and nephews (the children of her youngest brother) and her unabashed pride in their accomplishments infuse her story.

Elsie and I did not talk at length about her mother, as I did with Simone. But even though I asked Elsie about herself, Elsie's mother was present. Sometimes we carry the spirit of our mothers even if we don't openly express it. No doubt, individual stories and biographies have their own distinct character and contours, yet the individual story resides relationally, as if mothers' stories extend through the next generation, even after the mothers' worldly parting.

Elsie's mother penetrated her story both quietly and not so quietly. At dramatic moments, Elsie became her mother, such as when she heeded her mother's dying wish that Elsie tend to her ill father. It may be that Elsie continues to honor her mother's wishes today. At the end of our second interview, Elsie said that her mother would be pleased about her visits to Lebanon to meet family members there. "My mother would probably be tickled to death, real happy that I went there and met them." At that moment, Elsie's story made sense: Elsie is the family's history keeper. She is the family memory, connecting to the past. And in embodying the past and the present, she respects her mother. She is clearly situated between two worlds: the one her mother and father brought her into, as couched in the Lebanese community, and the contemporary one, where intermarriage is the norm. Elsie actively personifies the past and present through her maternal role. She is the treasured elder to five nieces and nephews and their children. "Yeah, if I ever married, I wanted to have children, but now I've . . . inherited five of them. My brother had five children, and that's all I have today is my brother's children. They all come to visit me and call me. I'll tell you what, I'm getting all these great-nieces and -nephews."

Many elderly people tell their narratives in the context of the past, not the present. But Elsie's story is decidedly intergenerational and situated between the worlds of yesterday and today. Here, Elsie's tale is told as it connects to her mother, who was of Lebanon but embraced Louisville and the entrepreneurial opportunities it offered, and whose children were not only physically but also spiritually part of her. It could be that the conduct of the daughter's life continues conversations once had with the mother. Elsie's large extended family would please her mother, who mourned the children she lost. "She had twins between me and my youngest brother," Elsie said, "and they died. I don't know what it was. She had mostly miscarriages, so one time she told my youngest brother (he's the only one that had kids), she said, 'I lost five kids after you were born.' And he said, 'I gave you five grandchildren.' . . . If all her children had lived, she would have had twelve." Elsie is connected to her mother in many ways: through the children of later generations, through the Lebanese friendships she maintains today, through her interest in Lebanon and her mother's relatives there, through her working life, through her continued association with the Orthodox church her father helped found, and through her maternal ways.

Elsie's story and, even more directly, her mother's story can be understood in terms of a correspondence between Lebanon and Louisville. Elsie's Lebanese father and his family were the first to immigrate to Louisville. Her father spent some of his childhood in Louisville, but he and his mother returned to Lebanon because she feared the impending war (World War I). Elsie's paternal grandmother was a mother alone in uncertain times. Elsie's father "was like five or six" when his own father died. "My grandmother brought him over to Louisville. He sold newspapers on First and Jefferson. They kept talking about a war, so my grandmother took him back to the village where my mother lived." There, Elsie's parents married and decided to move to America. "He and my mother married three months after World War I. They lived there [in Lebanon] a couple years. They had a little girl, and she died over there, so they decided to come to America. They came over then because there was nothing at that time; there was no work in Lebanon."

Despite Elsie's mother's promise to her own mother that she would return to Lebanon someday (see chapter 1), Elsie said, "In fact, my mother didn't want to go back. She liked the conveniences here." Elsie's mother told her four children born in Louisville that it was best to relegate Lebanon to the past and commit to America. She advised them, "'We're living here. We're not going back there to live.' My mother said her mother and father were dead. What's the use of going back?"

Yet in the 1970s, long after her parents had died, Elsie visited Lebanon. The place is significant to Elsie because it is where her parents came from and because she wants to maintain connections with her family's native land. There is something maternal about keeping and tending to the family's history—one's maternal history in particular—so that it is alive and present. Unlike Elsie, her three brothers showed no interest in traveling to Lebanon; however, one of them encouraged her to accompany other Lebanese people from Louisville who made the trip, even though it would leave him shorthanded in the family store. "My brothers never went. They didn't care to go. I went in 1970. . . . See, at that time a ticket was $300 round-trip, and some people from Louisville were going. I told my youngest brother, I said, 'I'd like to go.' He said, 'Go on.' I said, 'Who's going to help you?' He said, 'I've got these kids.'"

When Elsie arrived in Lebanon, there were family members waiting for her, including her mother's brother. Elsie's uncle would not leave the airport even though her plane was very late. "Our plane was seven or eight hours late," she recalled, "and my uncle, the priest there, he waited there. He would not leave. They said, 'They'll call you.' He said, 'No, I'm not leaving here without her.' He stayed there waiting for me. When I got off in Beirut, [a fellow traveler from Louisville] says, 'Elsie, there's your uncle.' My uncle said, 'I can't believe you're here.'"

Elsie made subsequent trips to Lebanon, but today, she no longer desires to return. "I loved going there with this other Lebanese lady. But right now, I'm too scared to go." Her nieces and nephews (whose mother was not Lebanese) and their children, meanwhile, are disconnected from the country, and they have expressed no interest in visiting Lebanon. "They don't want to go," Elsie said. "No, they never really wanted to go." This is the case even though her nieces' and nephews' Lebanese background is, at times, obvious. "My nephew that's a stockbroker, he went to

Sweden, and he took his wife with him. While he was there, a man says, 'Are you Lebanese?' And my nephew said, 'My daddy was.' And he said, 'I thought [so] by the name Nasief.'"

Unlike her nephew, who happened upon a Lebanese connection while traveling, Elsie traveled specifically to kindle Lebanese associations—associations that linked her to unsuspecting locales and infamous characters. Her uncle in Lebanon led a noteworthy life because he spent some time in Cuba. "See, my uncle lived in Guantanamo Bay, Cuba. . . . He worked for the American government; then he went back home, back to Lebanon." Elsie feels some kinship with Ecuador too, because she also has family there. One relative in Ecuador was legendary for his political escapades. "Okay, he wanted to run for president of Ecuador. Why they [his family] went to Ecuador, I don't know. When their father died in Lebanon, their mother took them to Ecuador. . . . Yeah, this guy, I have a lot of clippings on him. I visit[ed] with them. He had a dual, a fight with the president. All these [stories] were in American newspapers. That's how I got them."

Why did Elsie feel the need to continue far-off familial relationships while her brothers did not? I don't know for sure, but it seems that Elsie's desire to maintain past traditions and family ties comes from nostalgia or maybe even habit. She has chosen this path. Being part of the Lebanese community in Louisville is what she has always known.

When Elsie's parents came to Louisville sometime around 1920, they lived in proximity to family and friends from the same and nearby villages in Lebanon. "A lot of the people at church, their parents, grandparents, are from the same place as my mother and daddy are from, the same village. In fact, one of my real good friends, she and I played together, her mother and my mother played together in Lebanon." The Lebanese who settled in Louisville also started their own Orthodox church. "They had the church on Jefferson Street, and they would go there and they had dinners and [would] sell tickets and help fund the church. They were the founders of that church. We have a beautiful church." St. Michael's remains a staple in Elsie's life and is discussed later. First, I describe the Louisville that Elsie's mother encountered and Elsie knew—a Lebanese community that (like the Jewish one Gishie and Simone identified with) evolved from a cohesive group with few resources to a diffuse but more financially sound entity.

The Haymarket section of Louisville, ca. 1920s. (University of Louisville Archives.)

A couple of years after World War I, Elsie's parents arrived in Kentucky. "They stayed with my daddy's cousin," she said. "He lived on Wallace Street in Louisville. My daddy worked as a busboy in Seelbach Hotel. He made a little money, and then they got a room where all the Lebanese people had one or two rooms [in an] apartment complex. They opened up the fruit stand. And then my daddy opened up a little meat market on First and Jefferson. Then he moved back down by where the [fruit] stand was—there was an empty store. [He] and my uncle, [who] was married to my mom's sister, they opened up a meat market, and we were there for sixty-eight years." The family store stood in the Haymarket section of downtown Louisville for all those years. Today, the Haymarket is only a memory. Photographs chronicle how this part of town, from the late 1800s to the 1960s, was a vibrant merchant area where Lebanese, Italian, and Jewish immigrants sought to make a living. It is wistfully relished by some, while others unsentimentally relegate it to the past. For Elsie, who is not at all maudlin, it is simply the place where the family lived among other immigrants. "Well, there were Italians, Jews, and Lebanese. Yeah, most of the Lebanese, Italians, and Jews lived down there by the old Haymarket."

In the Haymarket, divisions between work and family blurred; immigrant families lived above their stores, and all family members assisted in the family businesses. Unlike in Lexington, where Jews stuck together in a nonimmigrant Christian setting, in Louisville, various immigrants resided together comfortably. Elsie's mother even developed a mother-daughter relationship with a Jewish woman. This woman "had three sons and no daughters," said Elsie, "but she loved my mother like her daughter. She said, 'You're my daughter.' And when my mother would get a customer, one of [the woman's] sons would go out and wait on them. Oh, they treated my mother so good, treated my mother very good."

Inevitably, tucked into many nostalgic stories told by Arab and Jewish immigrants are hardworking and determined characters, and Elsie's mother was one of these individuals. "My mother, she couldn't read or write, but she worked, gave change, and then later on when my daddy turned the business over and my brothers took over, he opened up a grocery store on the corner, and my mother helped him sell whiskey. She couldn't read, but she knew just where the bottle was."

Elsie's parents were determined to provide for their children, which included passing the meat market business on to them—but only to the boys. Elsie understood that the business would go to her brothers and not to her. "Oh, my daddy told me, 'I love you more, but you might get married and bring your husband in here to work and come between your brothers, and I don't want that,' so that was okay [*laughing*]." Although Elsie had resigned herself to her father's business logic, which excluded girls, she also understood the position of Lebanese girls and verbalized her displeasure to her mother. "I used to tell my mother, 'Lebanese people don't like girls; they like boys!' I just used to get mad and tell her that. She said, 'No, that's not so.' I got mad at her; she and I had a few words." Maybe Elsie's words got through to her parents, because they also saw to Elsie's well-being in ways that defied accepted gendered customs.

Elsie's mother and father insisted that Elsie be the executor of their estate, despite traditions that barred girls from such affairs. "I learned that a lot of Lebanese people didn't leave anything to the girls. They'd leave everything to the boys. Well, not my family. Everything was [split] four ways; in fact, I was executor of my mother's and daddy's estate. I was executor, and my mother and daddy said, 'Come on, we're going to a lawyer.' I said, 'What for?' They said, 'We're going to a lawyer.' They went to this lawyer, he was a Lebanese guy. They made me the executor of the estate. [My mother] said, 'I don't want a sister-in-law to kick you out of the house, kick you out of the business. You're my daughter. They're not my daughters.'"

Elsie's mother also blocked attempts to marry her daughter off. "When we were younger, some of them were still arranged marriages. They tried [that with] me, but I said, 'That's out.' Yeah, there was a guy my uncle wanted me [to marry], until my mother said, 'I want her to marry who she wants to marry. If she wants to marry him, go ahead.' My mother said to my uncle, 'I'm not telling her nothing.' And my mother didn't say nothing and said, 'It's up to her.' But I wasn't really interested in him at the time. I was young, but I'm not sorry." Today, she does not regret passing up that marital opportunity because her intuitions and resolve proved to be correct, as backed up by the friend who eventually did marry the man. "He had to look for a wife, but one of my friends married him. She said, 'You should have married him.' I said, 'No, I saved him for you,' 'cause he didn't treat her great. . . . He died. Her and I are real good friends. We still are."

In addition to leaving them a business, Elsie's parents tried to ensure their children's well-being by anticipating their future mobility. They purchased property in a neighborhood in Louisville not associated with "foreigners," with the intention that all their children would live there together. "My daddy bought the front property and then the house. . . . That way, my mom said, 'All [the kids will] get married and live next door to each other, and everybody will be close to everybody.'" The property was also purchased to give Elsie and her brothers the possibility of additional rental income. Elsie described the neighborhood her parents chose: "This neighborhood is a real old neighborhood with no Jews or Negroes or foreigners allowed to live there—they [the residents] didn't want them. They didn't really say much, 'cause we didn't really associate with them, but I'm sure deep down the older people didn't like it, but now it's okay. We've got a black couple lives across the street, and I have rented to a black tenant, so this generation [it's] okay. They don't care because we are all God's children."

Her parents' efforts worked. Elsie and her brothers put down roots in the neighborhood and worked in the family's meat-processing business and grocery store. Elsie worked there from the time she was fourteen until she was in her sixties. "We all worked in the store," she said, even if they had other aspirations. "Well, I always wanted to be a movie star when I was younger," Elsie remembered. "I would have liked to have gone to California or Hollywood or New York, but I stayed home. . . . I went to work in the store when I graduated from Atherton. It was an all-girls school then, and I just worked every day over there in the store." Elsie is not effusive when she speaks of the store. It was what it was. "We had the meat side over here and the grocery side over here. It was long, and in the back we had a kitchen and bathroom, two restrooms—one for the men, one for the women, you know. It was nice in those days, but it's nothing compared to stores today." She checked out customers and stocked the groceries. "Well, I'd wait on customers or give change, something like that. Yeah, wash shelves off and, yes, yes, it's a different kind of life now [*laughing*]."

It was a modest place, but Elsie considered it home; it was a place where she could pursue her love of college basketball and mingle with the regular customers. "I always felt like it was home there. Checking out customers, I enjoyed that, and I knew a lot of them that would come in; they'd come in all the time. . . . They were very nice and friendly. . . . I was a U of K [University of Kentucky] fan, [and] they were all U of L [University of Louisville] fans." The meats they sold met their varied customers' appetites and needs. "We had wholesale meats, and at one time we had thirty Chinese customers. . . . They had restaurants. We had a lot of black customers. We used to sell stuff that they would eat, like lamb, pigs' stomachs. And we sold shoulder bones, spare ribs—oh, around the Derby, we couldn't keep spare ribs in the store—and oxtails (they'd make soup out of that) and hogs' stomachs, all of that stuff. They'd buy like pork, ground pork; we'd grind it for them. My brother would order things that they'd want. Well, they used to eat pork stomach, and they ate a lot of pork bones, neck bones, and things like that, and kidneys and liver."

Elsie was deeply ensconced in the business her brothers owned, so it's not surprising that she and her last surviving brother made the decision to close the store together. The Haymarket had lost viability in the face of suburban malls. "Business was getting bad on the Market and the old projects and fruit stands," Elsie said. "It wasn't like it used to be, so we decided to close it. Yeah, he told me one day, 'Elsie, I think we ought to close.' He and I were the only ones left, and he said, 'I think we ought to close the store; we don't need this,' and so we closed it. We really didn't have much business [at] that time. Business was dead on the Market." Economic realities had changed, and the next generation had pursued professional occupations. Even Elsie, who liked working in the store, enjoyed other activities, such as her numerous trips. "Yeah, I liked working there, and of course, that didn't stop me from getting away. I've been on ten or twelve cruises, and I've been to Lebanon four times; I've been to Ecuador." In the end, the business served the purpose her parents had intended: it established the family in America.

Elsie's nieces and nephews also took part in the family business. "My one niece, she came to work when she was sixteen at the store; she worked on Saturdays. She was cashier, head cashier. In fact, my nephew the stockbroker, [when] he was about eight or nine, he served my oldest brother cleaning cases; he paid him, and that's how he made his money. We all worked there." But Elsie and her youngest brother had higher aspirations for his children. They wanted the next generation to move beyond the family business. She told the tale of how her nephew the stockbroker became one: "He graduated from U of L with high honors and went in the navy for a year or a couple of years, and [when he] got out he was working in the store. My second brother . . . (he played the stock market all the time), but, anyway, he'd tell him, 'What are you doing working here? With all that education you have, go out and get you another job.' [My nephew] said, 'I don't know what I want to do.' [My brother] said, 'Why don't you go be a stockbroker.' He said, 'Well, how do I find out?' My brother said, 'Buy the *Wall Street Journal*.' So he bought a *Wall Street Journal*, and Merrill Lynch had an ad for a stockbroker. So he went there and took a test and he passed and they hired him. So that Saturday we were real busy in the store. They [representatives from Merrill Lynch] came down to meet us all, and they said, 'We don't hire everybody, but with this family background, your people have never been in trouble with the law and all you ever did was work.'"

Elsie proudly talks about the success her family members have enjoyed since the store's closing. Just like a mother would, she owns her nieces' and nephews' accomplishments. "They went to college, have a profession. [I] have another nephew who went to U of L, he's a dentist, and my youngest nephew . . . is in the construction business. My niece has one boy and two girls, and the boy and a girl graduated from U of K and the [other] girl will graduate in May from U of K. She made the dean's list. I couldn't believe it. Her mother said, 'I got a letter. She made the dean's list.'" Elsie is proud. Her home is filled with photos of her nieces and nephews and their children, and she fetched newspaper articles about her nephew the stockbroker to share with me, just as a mother would.

Elsie learned her maternal ways from her mother. Fortitude infused Elsie's rendering of her mother; she was resolved that her children would be appropriately bestowed with material well-being. But she was also spiritually and religiously committed to her children. Elsie's mother was a religious person. As Elsie noted, her parents came from an Orthodox village in Lebanon, but those from "the next village were Catholic; they're from over there where Danny Thomas is from. The only difference in our religions is our priests marry, their priests don't. And when you read about all these priests, you think, now, it's a good idea to get married." St. Michael's Orthodox Church and the church community figured large in the family. "My daddy was one of the founders of that church. That's on my family history here. But a lot of the people at church, their parents, grandparents are from the same place as my mother and daddy are from—the same village." Her mother, along with other women in the community, raised funds for the church and managed church functions. "They used to have dinners, and the ladies would cook, do all the cooking, [to] raise money for the church." Her mother was devout. Before the Orthodox church existed, she frequented the Catholic church close to Haymarket for daily prayer. "There was a Catholic church a couple blocks away, and she'd go there," Elsie recalled. "My mother used to go to this old Catholic church; she and this other Lebanese lady would always go there." Religious commitment was deeply ingrained in her mother's family. Elsie's maternal grandfather was a priest, as was her uncle. When difficulties arose, Elsie's mother turned to religious and cultural practices for support.

Profound worry consumed Elsie's mother when her sons were stationed overseas during World War II. "It was right around Thanksgiving Day," Elsie remembered, "and we lived on top of the store then. My mother went to visit somebody, and everybody was listening to the Male Immanuel football game, 'cause that used to be real big in Louisville. She couldn't stand it. She said, 'I had to come home.' [She] came home, [and] my daddy was listening to the game. She went in the room and closed the door, 'cause she [was thinking] about my brothers. They were all in the service." It's almost as though her mother had a premonition of trouble. A day after Thanksgiving, the family received the news that one of Elsie's brothers was missing in action. Elsie was working at the store, and she had gone in the back. "My girlfriend was there and my [other] brother—he'd gotten a discharge—he was there, and I went back to get something and I came out. I said, 'What's the matter?' And they showed me the telegram that he was missing in action. . . . And [my mother] pulled all her hair out of her head. I was going around picking up hair."

Elsie's mother drew on her religion to cope with the situation. "Oh, my mother wouldn't have lived, but she made a pledge like they do in her country: if he'd come back, if we'd get word that he was okay, she was going to walk to the church barefooted. Well, it was a cold November day, and the lady that used to clean house for them, iron, would sit with her, and she said, 'Elsie, go to church and light a candle.' So I went to the church, [and while] I was there, they came and got me: we had a telegram; he's okay. . . . My mother walked to church barefooted." In the physical and spiritual world, Elsie's mother personified maternity to her metaphysical core. Elsie was in the shadows providing maternal support.

Lebanese women devoted themselves to their families, and Elsie's mother did the same. She cooked Lebanese Sunday dinners, she quilted bedspreads for each of her children, and she crocheted. She also unconditionally tended to her husband when he was ill, maybe even at her own expense. "My daddy had hardening of the arteries," Elsie said, "and my mother took care of him. She wouldn't let anybody take care of him but her. And she told me one time, she said, 'He's my whole life.' She said, 'I was just a little young girl from the country, and he's my whole life.'"

In some sense, as the only daughter in the family, Elsie was expected to take up the responsibilities associated with maternity. Most poignantly, this included taking care of her father upon her mother's death. "She [her mother] died in my arms. Last thing she said, 'Take care of your daddy, Elsie.' We never told him [she died], but he stopped asking for her and would ask for me, you know, being the only girl. . . . So I slept [in his room and] . . . he held my hand all night. Being the only girl, everything falls on you. And then he died two weeks later. My mother was fifty-eight and my daddy was sixty-two."

When their parents died, Elsie and her brothers carried on as expected of them. The family stayed together, and Elsie and her one unmarried brother arranged their lives around each other. "After my parents died, we lived together, just me and him. We put up this apartment complex here across the street. I lived in one and he lived in one. Our parents left us four lots, each one [got] a lot. . . . My youngest brother's kids wanted to stay in this neighborhood, so he put [up] a house." After Elsie and her brother settled in together, Elsie tried to do the things her mother would have done, like cook Lebanese dishes, but she had her limits. "The Lebanese people eat lamb's stomachs. I cooked [it] one time after my mother died and I said, 'This is it!'" Although Elsie draws the line at lamb's stomachs, she happily accommodates her nieces and nephews when they voice an interest in Lebanese food. "Let me tell you, my one niece loves rolled cabbage. We always had Lebanese food on Sunday. My mother would [cook on Sundays], but nobody comes over and eats anymore, but they all [Elsie's nieces and nephews] love rice. I make it with butter, salt, and pepper. They all love rice. Oh, on Sunday when we go to my niece's house that has the swimming pool, I'll take Lebanese food over there. That's what I can serve."

As the family's maternal figure, Elsie worries about everyone's well-being. One day in 2006, a plane crashed in Lexington. That same day, her nephew and his wife were expected to be flying into Louisville, and she feared that they were on the deadly flight. "They were coming home, and I knew they were due in, and I heard [about] this plane crash. I said, 'Oh my God.' Oh, I just walked around this house and I was just crazy. I hoped they weren't on that plane." Somehow, the image of Elsie's mother pulling her hair out comes to mind. Elsie's intense maternal feelings also caused irrational behavior, given that there was no danger to her loved ones: the crash was in Lexington, not in Louisville, and it involved a departing plane, not an incoming one.

Just as her mother sought comfort in the church, so does Elsie. She has remained with the Orthodox Church, even though her brothers did not. "No, they wouldn't go like I would go. My other niece is close to our church; she lives closer to church. [Other relatives] don't go to the Orthodox church. I'm the only one. I try to go every Sunday." Some relatives have become Catholic rather than Orthodox. "My cousins, they became Catholic, all five girls, they were all Catholic, and I have another cousin from Lebanon, Kentucky, she's Catholic." Elsie remains committed to the Orthodox church her parents founded, even as younger members of the family depart. Her nieces and nephews facilitate Elsie's desire to go to church but do not go themselves. "Now, if I want to go, I don't drive at night. One of my nieces will come pick me up and they'll bring me home. They don't stay."

Things have also changed at the church: the congregation is no longer solely Lebanese; there are now Russian and Ethiopian members, among other nationalities. Although Elsie is still closely associated with other Lebanese in her church, she is also in close proximity to Orthodox brethren of varied backgrounds. "Ethiopian, African, all kinds of nationalities belong to our church. And there's this one black lady. One time I missed, I missed that weekend, and she says, 'Honey, where have you been? I miss you.' All different nationalities, . . . but they're Orthodox, so you can't refuse them. It's a house of God, so you really can't refuse them, see." As is true for all of us, Elsie has had to negotiate change and acclimation.

What it means to embody a Lebanese American identity has altered. Elsie knows that her nieces and nephews and their children, as well as her friends' children and grandchildren, don't even think about marrying within the Lebanese community. "That's old-fashioned," she admits. "In fact, my friend, a Lebanese lady that I went to school with and go to church [with], and her grandson—well, he's not Lebanese, half, part Lebanese—he's going to get married, and the girl isn't Lebanese, and they're getting married in Jamaica."

Maybe Elsie was caught between marital traditions. She refused an arranged marriage and saw her other marital prospects as limited. The

Jewish woman who loved Elsie's mother might not have loved the idea of her Jewish grandson marrying an Orthodox Lebanese girl. "They [Elsie's mother and her Jewish friend] didn't stay in touch. . . . They [the Jewish family] had a grandson. He'd come in the store, and I'd always talk to him. They were afraid he was going to marry me [*laughing*]. That's what my brothers all used to say, [so] . . . they put him to work in another store. 'They don't want him to come here because of you.' But we were just friends. We didn't go out or nothing. That's the way people were [in] those days."

Change is omnipresent. On later trips in the 1990s, Elsie encountered an Americanized Lebanon and even found a Kentucky connection. "The last time I went to Lebanon, I couldn't believe it. We were in Beirut and [saw] all these American restaurants: Hard Rock Café, Dunkin' Donuts, ice cream, a Chinese restaurant, Kentucky Fried Chicken, McDonald's. So we went in Kentucky Fried Chicken and told them we were from Kentucky. They didn't know what we were talking about. They didn't know." Elsewhere in Lebanon, Elsie found a shared appreciation of University of Kentucky basketball. "In fact, we went to see a friend's cousin, she was there in Lebanon, and this guy came up and he [had] graduated from U of K. He said, 'I turned on the television and saw that UK won the NCAA'—the last one they won! [They] all speak English. They're more Americanized than we are."

Just as bits of Kentucky reside in Lebanon, material remnants of Elsie's Lebanese mother and her mother's memory are being transferred to the younger generation. Those bits are sometimes appreciated, or they may be misplaced. A quilt her mother made was ruined in a basement flood. "She made each one of us a bedspread, and I gave mine to my niece, and their basement got water," Elsie said. "My two nieces, they want a serving dish, and they don't [come] with a set of dishes. They came over here, 'Oh, this is what I want.' I said, 'What!' I had a bowl that belonged to my mother. 'This is what I want. I can't find them. We've been all over looking for serving dishes.' I said, 'Take what you all want.'" Relics from the past that are honored, cherished, desired, or even ruined represent the twists and turns of being Lebanese today among persons with distant Lebanese relations. When Elsie's nephew encountered that Lebanese man in Sweden, the nephew told him about a food memory involving his aunt Elsie. "My nephew said, 'When I was a little boy, see, we make yogurt. We make it.' And I used to make it, 'cause his daddy liked it, and I would make it for his daddy, and we'd eat it at the store. He told that man, 'I remember my aunt counting twelve times.' You had to, you had [to control] the temperature. He told me, he said, 'I can remember you making that.' And that man told him that as soon as that job is up in Sweden, he's going back to Lebanon."

Amid a world of weakened identities, Elsie mentions a godchild who is trying to resurrect Lebanese institutions from the past. "The Lebanese country club, people don't go there anymore. Well, I guess they just have their own, people have swimming pools in yards, and my godchild, he's trying to get the club back together."

TIED STORIES

Ethnic or religious identities have become a choice for some, just as daughters may cherish or discard some of their mothers' ways. Irrespective of how a mother is viewed, whether her ways are emulated or rebelled against, it might be said that stories are expanded on in future generations.

In talking with Simone and Elsie, it is sometimes hard to distinguish whose story is being told: Simone's or Gishie's, Elsie's or her mother's. Mothers' tales are passed down through daughters. Maternal echoes, or ripple effects, linger. Individual stories are not told in a generational vacuum; they enmesh lives from different generations. Even if we don't become our mothers, our mothers are situated in our own stories. Mothers provide a backdrop that is consciously or unconsciously reproduced, modified, or willfully tossed aside.

In this chapter, Gishie Bloomfield and Elsie Nasief have been juxtaposed to show enduring maternal effects. Gishie had children but did not follow maternal expectations for Jewish women of her generation. Elsie never had children, also failing to adhere to the maternal creed of her day, but she brushes aside this fact, gladly assuming a maternal role for her nieces and nephews, just as her mother would have done.

Gishie and Elsie negotiated maternal roles in social settings that almost mirrored each other. Their communities were nearly exclusively either Jewish (in Lexington) or Lebanese (in Louisville). These were Old World communities reproduced in the New World. Gishie's Lithuanian roots found new soil and form in Lexington. Lebanese Orthodox villages came to life in Louisville. Jews and Arabs mostly stuck with their own: outsiders were relegated to the background. What's interesting is that for both Gishie and Elsie, much of their community life was transmitted through their mothers. The family store that Gishie and Julian cultivated belonged to Gishie's family. Elsie spoke most noticeably of friends and family members related to her mother. Pain infused their families' stories of distant lands, and, correspondingly, former places were consigned to the past. Yet the past was revisited, as evidenced by Elsie's visits to Lebanon and Simone's trip back to Germany with her father.

In this country, work was what counted most. For Gishie and Elsie, work involved businesses that were not fancy or glamorous but simple and unadorned. These businesses were something for the later generations to embrace, but also to let go. Unlike the Myers sisters and the Isaac family, whose businesses lost a certain elegance as the generations advanced, in Gishie's and Elsie's families, the illustrious accomplishments have occurred mostly in later generations. Simone said it succinctly when asked about the possibility of her and her sisters' children working in the business: "Our kids are professionals."

Both families, equipped with gritty determination, used similar means to achieve financial stability, through investments in property and stocks. But while they were trying to ensure financial security for the family, other things were lost. Jewish and Arab identities were challenged. This weakening of identity mirrors how Jewish and Arab communities diminished as more of their numbers moved into the professional classes. Class mobility and suburban relocation certainly brought more comfort and status to these communities, but also less cohesive existences. At the same time, there are occasional hints that some are trying to resurrect the past. Examples are Elsie's godchild who wants to reinvigorate the Lebanese country club and myself in pursuing this project, which brings attention to women's past lives—in particular, those who lived and mothered on their own terms.

Fundamentally, the lives uncovered in this chapter were quiet ones. Gishie and Elsie were not community leaders, as Sarah Myers was and Teresa Isaac continues to be. They were women who etched out identities that both did and did not conform to their community's standards. Gishie became a mother but rebelled against prevailing notions of how Jewish mothers act. Elsie, in the course of our conversations, did not highlight her life as out of the ordinary, except when it came to traveling to far-off lands to connect with family. But ever so slightly and shyly, she hinted at moments of not agreeing with the norms of the day that privileged males over females and pressured women to marry men who were not to their liking.

By enlarging lives that are not publicly noticed, one can see remarkable things, such as women who choose to conform and not conform to maternal orthodoxy in their own hushed ways.

4

INTO FOCUS

IN THIS CHAPTER, THE STORIES of Manar Shalash and Sawsan Salem, who are Muslim, are coupled with that of Renee Hymson, who is Jewish. Manar and Sawsan are in their forties, and each has four children. Renee is in her late seventies; she has grown children and grandchildren and was widowed not long ago. Why tell their stories together? The reason is simple: their stories are largely invisible.

Images of Muslims, particularly of Muslim women, abound. In the public eye, they are covered and relatively silent. Their choice of garb is a topic of discussion and even controversy, especially in western Europe. They are likely to seem foreign and exotic. Jewish women, by contrast, are more familiar to the mainstream and have become so ubiquitous in the public sphere that they fade into the tapestry of American women. Yet this was not always the case; their stories, too, were once invisible (and may remain so). Contemporary images and stereotypes fail to depict Muslim women like Manar and Sawsan as modern mothers trying to negotiate work, kids, and community obligations, especially in places like Kentucky. Manar manages the family cell phone business with her husband; Sawsan initially ran a Mediterranean restaurant with her husband and brothers but now works as a sales associate in a store not normally connected with Muslims: Victoria's Secret. The similar juggling act that Renee performed in the 1950s and 1960s went undetected by her contemporaries. In the popular imagination of those decades, the typical mother was a white, middle-class woman confined to the home; she was certainly not Jewish and employed in the shoe department of the family store, Hymson's Tots and Teens. To be sure, Manar and Sawsan emerged from a distinctly different background and live in a distinctly different milieu than Renee. Working mothers were not commonplace in Renee's day. Today, by contrast, working mothers are the norm, but Muslims are usually not construed to be among them.

I have told their stories together to make their invisible lives perceptible. Perhaps it is wrong to say that their lives are invisible. After all, ideals of the 1950s mother flourished. She hardly stepped outside the home, and she catered to her family's every whim. Likewise, today's Muslim woman is hypervisible and is construed to be silent and voiceless. Just as 1950s ideals veiled the reality of mothers who also worked, contemporary images of Muslim women conceal the very real and active lives they embrace. Ideals and stereotypes abound, but real lives can remain hidden.

Negotiating, managing, and *juggling* are verbs one associates with the life of a working mother. Renee, Manar, and Sawsan are like many other women; much about their lives is familiar and commonplace. They are not unlike the mother character in the film *The Incredibles,* whose defining quality is her nimble flexibility in coping with situations that come at her from all directions and angles. There is a sameness to their accounts of having to arrange their work lives to fit their children's schedules. "I go in from 10:00 till 2:30, 3:00 by the time I get out to pick them [her children] up," said Manar. Sawsan did the same when she worked in the family restaurant. "I used to work there in the daytime until the kids came back from school." Her schedule as a sales associate at Victoria's Secret still puts the family first. "Four hours a day, sometimes six. I work like maybe three to four days a week," she said. Renee escalated her work hours as her daughters got older: "When I started, I worked on Saturdays, and then I went to work four-hour days and then full-time."

These are women in motion, shifting gears from moment to moment, dealing with family and business obligations, and contending with the disappearing boundaries between home life and work life. Manar manages the family cell phone business with the aid of technology at home. Although she may not physically be at the business full-time, she still works full-time. "You have to keep track of every inventory in each store, and what was sold and what was not, and sometimes I bring work home

Manar Shalash in the kitchen with her computer. (Photo by Sarah Jane Sanders.)

with me because I don't have time to do it while you have customers coming and going, so I . . . work on it at home too, so I'm working full-time.
Actually, it is full-time, because it's not enough time."

Renee sometimes brought her kids to the store, stretching her work
hours beyond the school day. "When the children were in school, I could
go for a four-hour day, and [then] I would rush home, park the car in the
drive, and run to the front door. So I could work those hours while my
kids were growing up. . . . Sometimes I took my kids to work. They rode
up and down on the elevator or I put them in the Strand movie theater
right next door to my dad's store, and the usher was a friend of my dad's,
and he would watch the girls. It was ridiculous."

As multitaskers, these women must focus on work, with their children in the background, at one moment and then switch gears and tend
to a hungry household the next. The daily dinner routine and the question of what to make for dinner were ongoing struggles for Renee. "In
those days," she said, "grocery stores were not open at night, and you had
to cook at night. You couldn't go in and buy something already cooked,
that was number one, and number two, A&P [the grocery store], whatever it was—we all went to A&P—you had to cook it yourself. So my
average dinner was—the only thing I could do was, I had a grill outside,
and I always put hamburger or steak on, because that was the best I could
do fast. I guess to some people it would be a luxury, but to me it wasn't. I
would have rather made a big pot of soup."

Manar and Sawsan enjoy conveniences, such as twenty-four-hour
grocery stores stocked with ready-made foods and multiple restaurant
dining options, that were unavailable to Renee. Unlike Renee, Manar and
Sawsan prepare Middle Eastern foods alongside multicultural "American" dishes that cater to their American children's appetites. According to
Sawsan, "75 percent of my meals [are] Arabic." Emad, Sawsan's husband,
piped in, "Today was Italian." Sawsan continued: "After I come home
from my work, I start immediately cooking. By 6:30 I will be finish[ed]
with the dinner. Maybe one time a week, sometimes two times a week
[we go out to dinner]. My kids, they love the Olive Garden and they love
to go to Gattitown, Cici's Pizza, and Chinese, Japanese." Sawsan tries to
accommodate her children's food tastes, but for her, food also represents
a culture she wants to impart to her children. Manar also continues to

serve Middle Eastern food to her American children, even if it's not their favorite fare. "Sometimes my kids don't like the Arabic food that much. They like the pizza, spaghetti, the fast [food], but I can't always make just that. I try to make at least once a week or twice a week Arabic food. . . . It's not like they hate it [or] they will not eat it. No, it's like, 'Oh, we have to eat this again?'" These mothers' daily dinner plight is familiar to countless mothers of all sorts.

Despite the demands in the kitchen, these women want to work because it meets needs that cannot be satisfied at home. Manar is certain that staying home is not for her. "I like the customer service part. It's like I can't stay home. If you put me in the house and tell me to just work from the house, . . . I can't. I stayed one time when I had the last baby. I stayed at home with him for a while because he was breast-fed. I did not like that. I didn't like it. It gets boring, so I have to do something." Sawsan also enjoys interacting with customers, but she has an additional interest in working: easy access to fashion and shopping through her job at Victoria's Secret. "Yeah, I love it. You see everything . . . new. I don't take my check home. I take like perfume and clothes." Emad couldn't resist commenting: "Yes, it's definitely not an income builder for us. Lots of sales, bargains. Every day is a sale. What's the difference between yesterday and today?" Sawsan openly admits her love of shopping and her attempts to hide her habit from her husband. "I hide the bags when I come home every day or I let my kids take the bags and say, 'Hide them from your dad.' . . . Yeah, he doesn't like shopping, but he has a wife, [and] she loves shopping." For Sawsan, the lines between being a consumer and being a saleswoman are blurred. But as a habitual Victoria's Secret customer herself, she can advise customers based on her own experiences, and she has a devoted customer base in the Muslim community, with both women and men coming to her for fashion suggestions.

Renee didn't mention shopping as a motivation to work, but like Sawsan, she was driven by a fashion sense. In Renee's case, this would benefit both the business and the women who frequented it. "I liked the business, and if I worked it would—I don't mean to sound conceited—it would be a better business. I had different kinds of ideas than my husband, and I thought of what would really work. Mine were for women. All I wanted to do was to get women to recognize [that] instead of buying

Sawsan Salem's closet, with dresses from Jordan and boxes from Victoria's Secret. (Photo by Sarah Jane Sanders.)

a dumb shoe like an Aigner, [they] could always get a shoe that really fit. They were expensive, but they didn't care. They would say, 'We know that.' In the end, what would happen is that about a month later they would come back [and say], 'It [the cheap shoe] didn't wear.' . . . I felt like it was important for a woman to be there [at the store] mainly when it came to the purses. God, if I didn't like it, how could the customers?"

Permeable boundaries mark these women's work, family, and community negotiations. They are active community members who find comfort and a sense of belonging among others like them, Muslims and Jews. However, being an active community member also means extra work, additional obligations, and more juggling. Renee was well aware that she differed from the Jewish women who stayed home with their children and did things like bake cakes for temple functions; for her, this chore was an unrealistic demand, given her already busy life. "Some women said, 'Renee, you have to bring a cake for Friday night.' I said, 'I can't. I'm working a six-day week.' They said, 'That's no reason you can't.' They never worked. It was so stupid. I wasn't mad at them. They had never worked, and they didn't know when you worked a six-day week and you have children to be with and help [with] homework and so forth, that you don't have time for something like baking a cake. I would have been happy [to do it] if I could have. . . . I don't think it was [meant to be] really mean. I just think they didn't know." Renee understands that others of her generation of Jewish women embraced their middle-class status by not working outside the home.

Manar, in contrast, does not speak of unrealistic requests. Instead, she describes her work in the Muslim community, including building the Islamic school that her two younger children attend. Community engagement for her is an extension of her mothering because she wanted her younger children to avoid the fragmented educational experience of her two older children. "Really, we [she and her husband] were the ones that helped organize the school, so we were the ones that were for it, because we wanted them [her children] to learn the Arabic, we wanted them to learn Islamic studies. My two oldest, we never had that school before, so I used to take them to a private teacher to teach them the Arabic and the Islamic studies, but it was kind of hard to do that just them by themselves. So I felt how they suffered. Right now, to be honest, my son, he doesn't know that much reading and writing Arabic; just basic he knows. He doesn't read it very well. My daughter, she's learning it in college now, the Arabic; she loves it, and I'm proud of her because she put whatever she learn[ed with] the private teacher and whatever she learn[ed] in college, and she's picking [it] up, so she's doing good with it. So with these two, the little ones, any Arabic book you open, any page for them—they're in the sixth and eighth grade—they can read anything, so I'm proud of that."

Religious obligations also exist in Manar's daily life. For example, she snatches moments to pray five times a day, and in fact, her prayer alarm went off during our conversation. "We pray five times, so it's like in the morning, early sunrise; and then the noon prayer; and then the . . . afternoon prayer; and then after sunset; and then the last one like around nine o'clock. That's the five of them that we have to do, five prayers. But we have a period for each one, when we can do it—like the morning [prayer can be done] until twelve o'clock, so we have time to do it. So this [her alarm] is an announcement to say, now it's the noon time or now it's the afternoon time to do it. So I have from now until sunset to pray this time. We have time [to continue the conversation]. It's just a reminder."

Although Manar and Sawsan are similar to other middle-class mothers in many ways, it is not the typical mother who works to guarantee that her children get an Islamic education or who incorporates five prayers into her daily routine. Manar and Sawsan are couched in the Muslim community first and foremost. Up to this point, I have tried to illustrate that much about their lives is familiar, maybe even mundane, despite public characterizations of Muslims as foreign and engaged in strange and alien ways. Manar talks like any other soccer mom. "I do soccer. They practice. Thank God, this year, this season it was both [of] them on the same day, . . . and I have people to take [one of the children], because I can't take both. I got [my son] a ride, . . . so we've got that taken care of. Games [are] on Friday and sometimes Saturday and Sunday, so really I get to do some laundry, some cleaning [on] Saturday—an hour here, an hour there."

The uniqueness of Renee's narrative rests in her commitment to other women, appreciating that her own biographical journey is indicative of larger social arrangements that limited opportunities for women and ignored them. Renee may have been more acutely aware of such strictures because she was in the business world at a time when most of her

Jewish peers remained in the home. A contemporary habit of thought deletes women like Renee from the public discussion by construing the overtaxed mother as a recent creation, not a long-standing institution.[1]

Manar Shalash and Sawsan Salem
Cell Phones and Lingerie
Lexington, Kentucky

One conversation with Manar and Sawsan does not translate into knowing their stories; instead, I can offer only a glimpse into their lives. My encounters with them in their homes were brief. I snatched an hour or so of Manar's time after three weeks of trying to make arrangements to meet her. She is simply too busy. I ran out to Sawsan's home and chatted with her and her husband, Emad, who is a first-generation Arab American and grew up in Cleveland, Ohio. "My dad actually served in Vietnam," said Emad. "He came here to go to school and got drafted." Sawsan and Emad warmly welcomed me into their home, even though I was a Jewish stranger and was worried about disrupting or disturbing boundaries.[2]

I am grateful to Manar and Sawsan for allowing me enough of an opening into their lives to know that public and popular portrayals of Muslim women both overseas and in the United States neglect the diversity of the lives they lead. The image of a covered and cloistered woman certainly does not apply to Manar and Sawsan. They lead contemporary lives in an unlikely setting (Kentucky), far from the urban locations where most other Muslims and Muslim Americans have settled.

Manar and Sawsan acclimated long ago to the United States and to Kentucky. They came to America as young women and new brides, following their Palestinian American husbands who happened to meet their wives in Palestine. Twists and turns involving movements among Jordan, Palestine, Brazil, and the United States mark their families' biographical maps. Manar speaks about her husband's family's multiple journeys. "His dad is from a village close to Ramallah [Palestine], like twenty minutes away. His mom is Lebanese, and his mom and dad met in Brazil; that's where his dad was originally, in Brazil. His dad moved from Palestine to Brazil and worked in Brazil, and that's where he met her. So they came here to Lexington, and they've been living here all this time. My husband came to the United States when he was ten and stayed here all his life in Lexington." Can it get any more confusing? Manar's Lebanese mother-in-law was Christian and remained Christian until recently, even though she raised her children as Muslim. Then, after forty years, she converted to her husband's and children's religion. When Manar's (future) husband was deemed to be of marrying age, his father took him to Palestine to look for a wife. "He came to visit, him and his parents, to Palestine in 1984, and his dad was pushing him to look for a bride, and he does not want to do that. He had a girlfriend here [in Kentucky], and he was having fun; [he didn't] want to get married. Then we met over there." Manar's and her husband's life paths reveal the multipart routes they traveled as people simultaneously of Palestine, America, Lebanon, and Brazil.

Sawsan's family originally hailed from Palestine, but they moved to Jordan with the onset of war. Later, half the family returned to Palestine, while the other half, including Sawsan's mother, stayed in Jordan. Sawsan's maternal grandparents went back to Palestine, "but [my mother], she married my dad and she stayed there" in Jordan. Connections to Palestine remain, however, and like Manar, Sawsan met her future husband in Palestine. "I got married. I met my husband in Ramallah. He came to visit Ramallah. I lived originally in Amman, Jordan, and we met like a couple of times, and then we married here in the U.S."

Clearly, Manar and Sawsan and their families maintain real ties among Palestine, Jordan, and America. Some family members still live in Palestine, and others are relocating to Palestine after spending years in America. Emad said, "My sister recently moved back to Palestine with her husband. Yeah, they got to the age, and her husband's an attorney; he decided it's enough of the United States, go back, raise his kids back in the country." Manar's four siblings live in the United States, and their mother divides her time between the Midwest and Ramallah. "It's just uncles who I have back home," said Manar, "and my mom, really. My mom, she lives most of her time in Ramallah. She just comes here for two or three months, four months, goes back, and then comes back here. She said, 'I can't stay here. I've got to go to my friends and my family.' She loves it over there. . . . [If] she wants to go to the market, she walks there. Everything is close. All her friends live around her, so over here is different. [Here] she needs someone to take her. Somebody to bring her. She doesn't drive. She barely speaks English."

Palestine and Jordan are omnipresent in Manar's and Sawsan's lives. Manar told me, "I always think about Palestine. I have a lot of friends over there. I have a lot of relatives. I keep in touch with them, and so it's nice. I would love to go every year if I had the chance. . . . I would love to go and take my kids every year just for them to see how it is." The homesickness was evident in Sawsan's words when I asked if she thought a lot about Jordan. "Yes," she said, "like when I hear someone is coming to visit and when its summertime, I always think about Jordan. It's so much fun over there in the summertime. We like going out, go to farms, and there is lots of party[ing] over there . . . and lots of people are outside. They come to Jordan, they live in a different country; everybody in the summer, they go visit. It's like a reunion in the summertime." Sawsan described a simple but rich life filled with outdoor gatherings in good weather, communing with friends, and eating fresh fruits and vegetables. "I miss my family and being around my mom . . . my friends. . . . The daily life, the shopping over there is different from here, but the food, we have everything, and we cook everything like overseas. The sweets over there I think [are] better [*laughing*]. It's simple over there, a simple life. Here, you have like a lot of stuff, like you have more expensive stuff, but it doesn't taste like overseas, like in my country. It doesn't taste the same."

Manar spoke of almost identical delights in Ramallah. "I love overseas. I love overseas. I love the weather over there. I love the social life. That's what I miss a lot. If it [were] in my hands, I would go every year, every summer." In particular, she misses the social life her children enjoy on overseas visits. "Here, . . . everything is available for them; over there, it's not. . . . They don't even look at TV that much over there. Kids will be outside playing with everyone; over here, all their time they spend either on TV or the computer or on the game cube. We take them to soccer; that's the only time that they really interact with kids. Overseas, when I take them overseas, I don't see them because they're always playing; they have something to do outside with the kids. That's what I love about it. Even here, with our neighbors, there are like two or three kids their age, but you don't see them much. You see them always inside, or they go knock on their [door], 'You want to play?' There's not a social life for the kids here, which I would love to see."

Sawsan Salem in her living room, surrounded by things from Jordan. (Photo by Sarah Jane Sanders.)

A full social life and plentiful fruit trees figure large in nostalgic and spiritual renderings of Palestine. You may recall Salim Natour from chapter 1, who, despite years away from Palestine, dreamed about his home and the numerous fruit trees there. "Over there," Salim said, the "weather is good. We didn't have like we have here, cold time weather, and in the summertime it [is] really very good. No rain in summertime over there. Fruit [has a] better taste than fruit here, because you get from the tree. . . . The store where they sell fruit, you could smell the fruit from two blocks, the apple, all kind of fruit, everything fresh—fruit fresh, vegetable fresh, meat fresh. You could go to the market every day and get fresh meat, fresh vegetables, fresh fruit. Everything is fresh over there. Here, frozen." He recalled that when his mother came to the States, she deemed the bananas here "just like potatoes" and asked, "'What kind of banana is this?' Over there, you could smell the banana from two blocks, 'cause over there everything [is] fresh. That's a big difference." Salim was a man in his seventies, and his mother was long dead, yet he still remembered his mother's evaluative gaze when she first settled in Kentucky in the 1960s. The consensus seemed to be that there is a spiritual connection between the fruit trees and home—something that cannot be reproduced in Kentucky.

Manar's words mirror those of Salim and his mother. "From the tree like the fig tree, the fig tree early in the morning, that's the best fiber you can have. You just pick it from the tree. Plums, we had plums. We had almonds. We had peaches. We had lemon trees and grapes around our house. I came here, I planted a fig tree. I didn't have figs [myself] overseas, but I had a fig [tree] across the street from a neighbor, but I planted here a fig tree. I planted a grape tree, but . . . I don't have the fruit from it."

Precious old-country charm mixes with more contemporary trends. Sawsan, as a fashion maven, misses the European fashions in Amman as opposed to the static Kentucky attire. "Yes, they have very nice stuff over there, very nice, more stylish. They have stylish stuff. Here, like most of the clothes are simple, classic. Over there, we have stylish clothes. Here, every year you could go to the mall and you see the same stuff every year, the same. I always ask my sister, 'What's the fashion this summer over there?' And after a year, it will come here, because they have clothes from Europe, Turkey, Italy."

Ramallah has undergone a transformation, reconfiguring it from a fruit tree–rich village to a modern capital city. When Manar returned to Ramallah, she found a landscape she no longer recognized, defined by dense urban sprawl. "It's not trees anymore. It's more houses, more story houses. Now, when I went four years ago, the [taxi driver] asked me, 'Do you know where you're going?' I said, 'Yeah.' No, I didn't. It changed so much on me that I did not know which street to take because the buildings went higher and there are more buildings now, [so] that I don't know if it is [the right] street. So we had to go all the way down, and then I told him, 'No, that's not it.' So he brought me back and we went to the next street and I said, 'Yeah, this is it.' It's really changed. I said, 'Oh my God, where's the trees? I don't see trees anymore.' People are like packed on top of each other, and [you have] to go higher to see the view, but the more you go higher, there's no view anymore." Jordan has likewise changed with the influx of well-to-do Iraqi refugees and the concomitant rise in the cost of living. There's "lots of Iraqis there," according to Sawsan. "There are lots of refugees from Iraq; they like triple the [cost of] houses over there. If you buy a house for $50,000, now it's going to be $150,000, because they've bought everything and they raise the [price of] houses and everything. Yeah, most of the people, they came to Jordan with money. All the big shots coming over there 'cause it was closer, and Jordan, it's open for everybody."

Sawsan and Manar take note of the changes in their homelands, but they have embraced Lexington and voice love for their adopted home. Manar said, "I love the United States; everything is easy here. Everywhere you go, you don't have to worry about checkpoints or borders . . . to get to somewhere. I came in 1985. I got engaged overseas, and [my fiancé] did the paperwork, and then we had the wedding here in Lexington. I love Lexington. I've been here since then. I've visited a lot of places, but I like Lexington. It's a nice city."

Similar words came from Sawsan and Emad. "My wife loves this place," he said. "This is a great city, very open. We never had any repercussions. Our neighbors are great; we get along with them. They know our background." Sawsan and Emad previously lived in Cleveland and Chicago, big cities with large Palestinian Muslim communities, and they had some concerns about moving to Kentucky. "Now, when we first moved, we were scared just from the stereotypes that you hear from Kentucky, but not in Lexington." It may be that the city shelters them from difficulties that might lurk in rural areas.

Manar and Sawsan inhabit the same Muslim community in central Kentucky. It is a thriving, close-knit world dedicated to families. Sawsan and Emad described it: "I would say for us, . . . we're in a great area for our religion, because the community that we deal with is very religious, so we have a group that we network with, and it's good for the kids and they enjoy it. During our Ramadan we get together every week and break fast together. Everybody brings their families, so I think this city is perfect for our family. Yeah, in the *big* city, I never see that." An added pleasure in Lexington is that Muslims from a variety of nationalities coexist. Sawsan explained it this way: "In the big city, they tend to stay within the same, like Palestinian with Palestinian. You don't mix with other nationalities. Here, all the nationalities mix together. You will see a lot of nationalities if you go to dinner or some Muslim activity. You will see all the nationalities—Pakistani, Indian, Arab from Sudan, from Africa, Egyptian, Libyan, Palestinian—they're mixed together."

Life is good in Lexington, according to Manar and Sawsan. Discrimination is not a problem for them, but Sawsan has seen it affect her friends who cover their heads or wear the *hijab*. "For me, I didn't have no problem, maybe because I don't cover. I don't have a scarf. I've never had any problem, but I have lots of friends [who] cover, and they have lots of problems everywhere. Even some people, they just stick their heads from the car and they tell them, 'Go back to your country.' . . . [But] it doesn't affect me at all. I don't have anything to tell you about that." Manar said the same thing. "I don't wear the *hijab*. Maybe whoever wears the scarf, it's a different story, but I have nothing going on."

Because they do not display the outward markers of their religion, Manar and Sawsan escape discrimination and enjoy freedom of movement without probing gazes. They do, however, encounter misinterpretations of their racial or ethnic makeup. Most often, Latinos confuse them for one of their own. Manar has grown accustomed to Hispanic customers, among others (even other Arabs), coming into her cell phone business and thinking that she is Latina. Manar sometimes experiences the same confusion: "When [an Iraqi woman] walked in," she admitted, "I thought she was going to talk Spanish to me."

Manar Shalash in her cell phone business. (Photo by Sarah Jane Sanders.)

Encounters of a similar sort greet Sawsan at Victoria's Secret. "They think we are Spanish. . . . They come and talk to me in Spanish. No Spanish, Arabic." In the public sphere, Sawsan notices a difference between younger customers, who are genuinely curious about her background, and some of the older patrons, who may be distrustful. "In my work, because I have an accent, they always ask me, 'Where are you from?' The young ones are fine, but sometimes I have . . . the old[er] people, the ones who sometimes don't understand my accent. But the young ones, they understand and they talk to me . . . and they're interested. Sometimes I feel the old people—not all the old people—some people are racist. Some of them act weird when they talk to me or if I go ask them if they need any help, they don't want my help. Some of them, not all of them. I meet very nice people in my work." Fundamentally, Sawsan prefers not to dwell on the difficult interactions. "It doesn't bother me. Some people, they make it like a big deal. . . . Some people [are] racist and they talk about [it], but I'm saying fine, because if you see something different, some people ask, and I don't mind. They want to ask or know anything about me, but in a nice way."

In our conversations, the focus was not on social difficulties; as I said, Manar and Sawsan are happy in Lexington, and they are unmistakably experts at acclimating. They adjusted long ago to a new country, culture, language, and community; their arrivals in this country without language or family are distant memories. Manar had to cope with language gaps between her and her new husband. "I understand it [English] because I learned it in school, but we never had the [opportunity] to talk to anyone really. . . . [My husband would] speak to me in English, and I [would] respond in Arabic. He can understand Arabic. I was speaking in Arabic, and he was speaking in English, but that's how I learned English quick. In the first year, it's hard . . . . anywhere. . . . All his family was here, and . . . none of my family. His family has been very nice to me, and I lived with them for a month and a half when we came. Then we moved to an apartment; then when we had the first baby, we moved to another apartment; and then we bought this house. We've been here since [then], and it's going to be eighteen years we've been in the same house."

Manar found refuge at a church-run program for foreign and displaced women who were new to the United States. "Every Thursday they used to have a gathering for two hours, three hours. We [would] go meet over there. We put the kids in the day care. . . . We just loved to go because everyone was there, any country you think of, it's there. . . . [We would put on] a talent show; they have a stage, and everybody from their country, they [would] present what's [popular in] their country. We used to have so much fun with that. It'll be American, it'll be Jew, it'll be Pakistani, it'll be Indian, it'll be Egyptian, from all over. And they teach English. There's classes for English, classes for cooking. It's a group just for interacting."

Sawsan complements her regard for this country with one for her home in Jordan. "You know how people overseas, they dream [of going to] America. They think that America is like dreamland, [but] not that much [for me], 'cause I lived in Amman, Jordan. It's a nice country, and almost everything we have in this country, we have it over there." Sawsan has adjusted. "I just make new friends wherever I go. I make friends. I still remember my old friends."

No doubt, their moves from the Middle East to Kentucky are the biggest changes Manar and Sawsan have experienced, but they have also adapted to dynamic familial business and career shifts. Manar and her husband tried multiple business ventures before settling on cell phones. "Well, really, the grocery did not work out very well, so we were trying two or three store locations to see if it [would] work better, and it wasn't like what we hoped. But when we went to the Subway it was a little bit better, a little bit better business, and then we went to the cellular [phones], and it was cleaner too. We got away from the food, and the smell of the food. The hours [were better] too; by eight, nine o'clock we were home, but with Subway you have to stay until eleven, twelve at night, so it is hard. . . . We're still in the cellular [business]."

Sawsan followed the career and business initiatives of her husband, moving as his career changed from administrative work with an Arab American organization in Cleveland to corporate work in Chicago and then Kentucky. In Kentucky, they also opened a Middle Eastern grocery and restaurant to assist Sawsan's brothers, who were settling in the States from Jordan. Emad started the conversation about the restaurant: "We had a business here in Kentucky, a Middle Eastern grocery store. I started that up from scratch. I opened that up about five years ago, and last year I sold it. We did it as a little investment, because I have another job, so I just did it as an investment. I worked on weekends and at night. . . . Initially, her brothers came into town, and we opened the business to help them out 'cause they were just coming to the States. There were three of them, so that was part of the investment really, to help out family. Now they're situated and [we] sold the store. It was a good concept. We had food, and then we had groceries and fresh meats. It was unique; there was nothing else like it in Lexington."

Sawsan spoke of her place in the business. "I used to work there in the daytime until the kids came back from school. All nationalities. We had Indian, Pakistani, American, Jewish, Iraqi—different nationalities, different dialogue. I use to [handle] the meat and . . . cooking. We had a butcher shop inside. I enjoyed it, but I got tired at the end. [I] did lots of stuff with the employees, and it was a headache." Sawsan and Emad both laughed about Sawsan's shift from handling food to dealing in women's intimate apparel. Sawsan said, "I know [I went] from smelling like food to . . . " Emad finished her thought: "From coming home smelling like spices to coming home and smelling like perfume."

Perhaps Manar's and Sawsan's most exacting juggling act is making sure their American children identify with Palestine and Jordan, respectively, and with being Muslim. Success in this endeavor can be measured by whether their children marry Muslims. Lost heritage—a fate that befell earlier Arab American generations—is something Manar wants to avoid. "It's fading; they're not keeping up with the Arabic. They're not keeping up with their heritage, which [is] too bad." Emad expressed his goals in this regard: "I wanted to make sure my children, when I had children, would have that same heritage as well, so I wanted to go back overseas. And if you're going to maintain it, that's the way to do it, 'cause a lot of people were born here in the States. The culture kind of fades, the language has faded." The necessity of instilling a strong identity grows as their children become teenagers and young adults. Children, Sawsan said, "when they are young, they are 100 percent Arab and Muslim, but when they grow up, I feel like . . . they are American Muslim, Arab American. They will have the culture, both cultures." Outside influences start to matter. "It is very hard, 'cause you teach them something in the house, and they go outside and . . . the whole school [environment] is different." Sawsan and Manar, along with their husbands, are not passive in this regard; they take precautionary measures. Despite their children's protests, Sawsan and Emad send them to Islamic school on Sunday mornings "to learn their religion, to read and write [Arabic], from eleven to two." Sawsan is very pleased that the Muslim community in Lexington is oriented toward families and children's activities. "They have lots of activities from the mosque, and . . . they go to the ISCK, the Islamic Society [of Central Kentucky]. They have lots of activity for Muslim kids, and for the holiday they make a big party at Gattitown and invite the kids for free." Drawing on the Muslim community and speaking only Arabic at home are a couple of ways that Sawsan tries to instill a Muslim identity in her children.

Manar has gone further. Her two older children, who are now young adults, went to secular schools, and she had to piece together an Islamic and Arabic education for them. Her two younger children go to an Islamic school—an environment where they don't stand out, where they are the same as everyone else. "When we turn on the Arabic TV and they want to read the letters and the names, they [can] both read the names. I am so proud of that. I love it. So at least we got that done, and it's part of the school; everybody's doing it with them. They don't feel like they're differ-ent. What I'm worried about is the social life after they leave that school to go to . . . high school. That's going to be a challenge; that's going to be fun. My oldest one, he started second grade and the other one started first grade [at the Islamic school], . . . so they're [been] there and [will be among] the first graduates [who] went all the way through."

High school fills parents with dread, irrespective of their background, and this may be especially true for parents who are raising their children outside of the cultural norm. For Manar and Sawsan, return trips to Pal-estine and Jordan help. When I talked with Manar, she was planning a trip to Ramallah with her two youngest children. "Last time I went it was five years ago. I try to go every four or five years. It's expensive to go over there. I'm going this summer at the end of May. I'm taking the two little ones; the eldest, everyone has their own thing to do, so I'm just taking the little ones. I can handle the little ones. The big ones, they don't want to go with me. Everyone has their own life they want to take care of."

Overseas, Manar's American children have to negotiate being both of a place and not of a place. Her children's American social ways differ from those of Palestinian boys the same age. "The way they raise [kids] overseas, the kids, I noticed they socialize much better than we socialize here. Like [if] my son [were] to go over there and talk to other kids, they think he's not man enough to talk to them. So that's part of social [life] over there. They take care of themselves by themselves, but my kids are too [much like] babies for them. If we go to people's house overseas, their kids sit with us and they talk with us like they're part of the gathering, but my kids say, 'Do we have to do this?' [*laughing*]."

Foreign social practices are not lost on Manar's boys, and her youngest son voluntarily attended to guests on their last visit overseas, an activity that he neglects in the States. "Yeah, I love the way my little one, when I went last time, he caught [on] that when somebody comes into your house, you've got to bring something to serve them . . . water or coffee or something. So as soon as somebody comes in, he goes to the kitchen, [pours] cups of juice, and brings a tray, and he wants to serve everybody. He loved doing that. Why? I don't know. We've never done it here in this house. I do it usually, but he's never done it. But he picked it up over there, and he wanted to do it. It was really different. Why would he pick something like that to do, but over here he won't do it? It's not that he won't do it. It's that he doesn't think about it."

Manar's children are familiar with two worlds, but they are fundamentally American. "When we go there [to Palestine], it's fun, but I don't think they would like to live there just because they're not used to there, and all their friends are here. It's nice to go visit, but I don't think it's a good idea for them to go and live there, no. I don't think they would like that. I would love for them to go, but [*laughing*] it's different. When you are raised here, I think you would like [it] here; if you were raised back home, you would love to go back. It all depends where you were raised, where you spend more time."

Sawsan regularly takes her children to Jordan and has taken them to Palestine to visit family there, too. "Yeah, we went to visit over there like maybe four years ago, five years. I go to Amman like every two years, but I took them back to Palestine, showed them Ramallah." More frequent visits, especially during Ramadan, would also be to Sawsan's liking. "I wish I could go back [to] visit during Ramadan and have a holiday over there with my kids. Yeah, that's my wish. Ramadan comes when the kids are in school; this year it will come I think August 20, and every year it will come like ten days earlier. Maybe after five years or six years the kids will be grown up. I want to take them at this age [so] they will see stuff that's different when they are very young."

Unlike Manar's kids, one of Sawsan's daughters wants to move to Jordan and has begged her father (maybe in collusion with her mother) to sacrifice his well-paying job in Kentucky for one in Jordan with lesser pay. "Actually, my daughters would prefer living overseas than living here. Yeah, the one that was sitting over here, she's begging every day to go back and to live there, the twelve-year-old. I thought about it, but my husband doesn't want me to go there. He's against [it], 'cause he has . . . a nice job here. One time my daughter asked [him] to work like a taxi cab or do falafel [laughing]." A move is financially unrealistic, in Emad's estimation. "I told her I need a job. How are you guys going to survive? So she said, 'Drive a cab. We don't need a lot of money, drive a cab, drive a cab.'" A move back to Jordan will have to wait for the Salem family and would most likely entail splitting time between the Middle East and Middle America. Here and there, back-and-forth movement resurfaces.

Situated in Kentucky, Sawsan and Manar think about the marriage prospects for their high school– and college-age children, and overseas possibilities are certainly a consideration. It is on their minds, even if Manar's twenty-two-year-old daughter is not thinking about it. "Well, I was twenty, twenty-one when I had the first baby, but my daughter, now I tell her, 'When I was your age, I had you.' She's still not engaged or anything." And practices have changed since Manar married. Manar's husband, at the urging of his father, traveled to Palestine to find a wife. At that time, ideas about suitable mates were more entrenched, according to Manar. "He [her husband's father] was showing him the younger [girls]. Me and my husband are the same age, so he was showing him younger girls than him, but when he saw me, he told him, 'I want Manar.' Normally, they want to get married to somebody a little bit younger than them. When he came to ask for me, I said, 'He's too young. Why is he getting married now? He's my age.' . . . The girl [is] always looking [for a] guy . . . [who is] older than her to marry. . . . She doesn't want one like [the] same age or younger [laughing]. This guy is too young for me, but then he asked and I talked to him and we liked him. I liked him, and we got engaged there. And it was a quick thing, too."

Manar is fully aware that matchmaking practices of the past do not work today. "I know it's not going to be that easy. . . . The old generation, they think this is a great idea for people to meet, but your kid is going to meet [a potential mate] anywhere. It's not like if you take them; . . . it's not like before. It's getting different now. Everyone wants to meet and get used to it, [get to] know them very well before they get married. It's not like us before, matchmaking. It won't work."

It goes without saying that they want their children to marry someone Muslim. Manar was honest about her desires. "I prefer, I'm not going to lie to you, of course. I would love for them to be Muslim. I would love for them to be from Palestine also." But in Kentucky, are such expectations realistic? I'm not alone in asking this question. Sawsan's daughters query her, "'How am I going to marry a Muslim? How am I going to know him?' and stuff like this. Both of them [her two daughters], they want to know how they are going to get married to a Muslim." Sawsan sees opportunities at the university or through familial connections. "Even the college, they have like a group, a Muslim group, and they get together." Emad explained that local, national, and international connections also hold potential. "Who knows? It could be outside of the States when we go to another wedding. We still have friends in Cleveland; it could be a wedding in Cleveland or New York. The population is so big, usually you'll go to an activity or a wedding and they'll see your daughter or whatever, and they'll come up. They'll ask about the family. 'What do you know about these people?' We'll set something up. 'Can we go and meet them?' You'd be amazed. Here we are in Kentucky. I used to work in Cleveland, Ohio. I would know if somebody brought up a name, I might know somebody that knew that person."

Family guidance plays a role, according to Sawsan. Any prospective son-in-law would have to be approved by the family. Family reputation counts, and community members keep tabs on one another, Emad told me. "Well, I think that's what helps with us. We're maintaining the culture, maintaining the religion, and we put them in the Islamic school on Sunday so they understand why we do certain things that we do. You tie it all to the religion and the reputation, her and the reputation of the family."

In-group connections are maintained in the old country: Palestinians marry Palestinians. Egyptians stay with Egyptians. "Like in our country," said Sawsan, "you don't see a Palestinian marry an Egyptian. It would be strange." But Sawsan and Manar live in Lexington, which is more international. Sawsan continued her thought: "Here, . . . Palestinians, they marry Libyans, [they marry people] from Sudan, from lots of places, and it's normal because you don't have a choice. You don't have the choice to make. They marry sometimes Pakistanis, [who are] not even Arab, but they are Muslim." Manar hopes for a Palestinian husband for her daughter, but, she clarified, "It's not like I'm against anybody else, but I would say it's going to make their family a little bit broader to [marry someone] from a different country. It's nothing against Lebanese or Syrian or Egyptian; it's just if I need to take her back home [after she's married], she won't have the hassle of different countries. I cannot say no, and she knows I prefer a Palestinian."

Manar may or may not have to abandon her hopes for a Palestinian son-in-law, but if her daughter chooses a non-Palestinian Muslim, I suspect she'll be satisfied. Manar and Sawsan have lithely acclimatized themselves to changing situations and landscapes in the past: they've had to. They are present here and there, at various places in their work, family, and community lives, and unlike other contemporary American mothers, they maintain ties to homes elsewhere, ensuring that their American children identify with their native lands and cultures enough to marry Muslim. They, and others like them, differ from previous generations of immigrants who sought to shed the past. Simone's grandmother, Bube, couldn't understand why anyone would want to visit the old country. Elsie's mother told her children to focus on Louisville, not on Lebanon, because they were here, not there. Manar and Sawsan, in contrast, are both here and there simultaneously, building an attachment to the United States without relinquishing the one overseas.

Renee Hymson
Hymson's Tots and Teens
Lexington, Kentucky

How do Manar's and Sawsan's stories relate to that of Renee Hymson? Unlike the other women featured in this book, Renee doesn't speak of foreign lands and seems far removed from immigration—both her parents were born in St. Louis. Renee is a Jewish woman nearing eighty, while Manar and Sawsan inhabit a completely different generational and cultural context. Or do they? Renee's generation gave little thought to women's multiple responsibilities; multitasking wasn't a concept, like it is today. Moreover, the standard image of the ubiquitous multitasking mother leaves Muslim mothers out. Thus, Renee, Manar, and Sawsan are linked by the silence that cloaks their stories.

There are other unexpected similarities. The Muslim community Manar and Sawsan inhabit is not unlike Renee's Jewish community of the 1950s and 1960s, where people identified first and foremost as Jewish. Jews lived, worked, and prayed together. European immigrants from a variety of countries (like Lexington's Muslim community today) were an integral part of the mix. Another similarity is that Renee never had stereotypical Jewish looks. With her blond hair and smallish nose, Renee often had to convince others, even other Jews outside of Lexington, that she was in fact Jewish and had two Jewish parents. As a result, non-Jews spoke their mind about Jews in her presence. Likewise, Manar and Sawsan are often not recognized as Muslims, unlike their friends who don the *hijab*. Other resemblances among the three women involve physical beauty and a fashion sense that differs from the norm in Lexington. When I chatted with Renee, she was wearing a large pendant necklace of African origin.

There are additional commonalities. Both Manar and Renee married and had children at a young age. This precluded obtaining an education— something Manar didn't mention but was a central theme for Renee. Both made sure that their daughters were well educated: Manar's is a college graduate, and one of Renee's obtained her PhD. Renee has given educational opportunities for women considerable thought. "I felt so bad when a woman wanted an education. That was always really important to me, and there were so many women who took their education for granted. They didn't realize that there were plenty of women who couldn't get an education, and in my age bracket, seriously, there were a lot of women who did not go to college."

Of course, there are also differences between Renee and Manar and Sawsan. One is how they narrate their stories. Renee tells her story as part of a larger narrative about the position of women in America and in Kentucky. In Renee's assessment, things have both changed and stayed

A young Renee Hymson. (Courtesy Renee Hymson.)

the same for women. "I married him [her second husband] in '57. That's when I started [working] on Saturdays, and then I went to work four-hour days and then full-time, but that was part of the thinking of the time. . . . I actually believe that it is still happening today, because I talk to too many women, young women who are having the same problems I had" balancing family and work.

Renee was an eighteen-year-old bride from St. Louis when she followed her new husband to the Texas-Arkansas border. "A week after I was eighteen [I married] and moved to Texas. Before we moved, we had a lot of RCA color televisions in the garage. I could never figure [that] out. Well, they were cold sets, or hot—I don't know what you call them. They were stolen, and I didn't know that. I told all my friends, 'I don't know why he has all those sets in the garage.' And [when] we moved to Texas, it was a federal offense because he brought them over the [state] border. . . . [Later,] when I accidently found out the truth, I was so overwhelmed I took my two babies and a jar full of change . . . and clothes thrown in the car." She was a young mother trying to get her children to safety without the aid of a map to guide her to Kentucky (where her family had relocated) and with no previous experience driving on an interstate highway. She was a mother in distress fleeing a difficult situation.

Renee made it safely to her family in Kentucky and the Jewish community she knew. Connections with her husband evaporated; she heard only vague rumors of his subsequent pursuit of a career in education. "No, he did not support the children. It turned out that he went into education. . . . He never knew anything. I can't imagine what he taught. . . . But just like [he was] a con man with the color television sets, he could have been a con man [with] . . . that." In her estimation, he wiggled his way out of child support, and the Texas courts allowed him to do so. She asked her ex-husband for a dollar a day in child support. "When I went to the courts, the judge said, 'You can't accept a dollar a day.' I said, 'If it's two hundred a day, I'm not going to see it.' He said, 'You will. Go on to the higher courts in Dallas.' I said, 'I've gotta get home to my children. I can't be here. I can't afford to be here.' And so I went home [to Kentucky]. . . . [If I had] gone to the other court, it would have cost me a fortune to live in Texarkana in a motel till they took me, [and] what would I have gotten? Five dollars a day? . . . I didn't [even] get the dollar a day."

Renee's parents, though originally from St. Louis, had settled in Lexington in the late 1940s, readily integrating into the city's Jewish and wider community. Her father's sister and brother-in-law were already established in the women's shoe business, and her father extended the business to include men's shoes. Men congregated at her father's store. "My dad was in business, and his store was such a meeting place for the men. They all went there at lunchtime or when they had a break, and they would just sit and talk and enjoy each other. And one guy named Jeter, he worked for my dad and he drank a lot and he had a gun. My dad said to him, 'Let me take the gun. I'm going to put in the safe. You can have it back Monday when you come to work.' So he [Jeter] drank on the weekend. It was that kind of store."

When Renee settled in Lexington in the 1950s, Jewish-owned stores anchored a vibrant and active downtown. The Jewish community was familiar to her. Although she was the only divorcee among them at the time, she acted like the other Jewish women—carpooling, going to meetings, tending to her daughters—which kept her from standing out as different. "I didn't really have a problem because I took care of my kids and I drove carpool with all the other women, and I went to Hadassah [a Jewish women's organization]."

Renee was strapped financially and had to live with her parents, but members of the Jewish community came to her aid. The temple didn't ask her to pay dues. "At the temple, they were very nice; they never charged me for the children to go to Sunday school. I guess they thought it was part of my parents' membership."

Still, Renee was struggling. She couldn't afford cough syrup for her daughters. "Oh, my problem was cough syrup; that was my problem. You can buy it over the counter today. We gave all our kids Robitussin—that was a prescription. My kids always had a cough, and I remember calling the ex-family [her former husband's family] and saying, 'You've got to give me the money.' I couldn't go to the drugstore, and of course, they didn't [pay]." Maintaining a job wasn't economical, given the costs of child care. "I took them to nursery school back when I got a job. My mother picked them up, so I could get a job. They offered me a buyer's job. They only paid five dollars a day, [and] I paid five dollars a day a child, so I couldn't afford to work. I wasn't making that much myself, so that was another thing. They say that a woman needs to work. She needs to be able to keep the children."

Navigating the day-to-day hassles of children and work, Renee wasn't too focused on Cokie Hymson, an eligible Jewish bachelor nine years her senior. "I knew him. When I first came to town, he called and said could he take the kids for a ride? And I said [*laughing*], 'Can we make it a rainy day?' I don't know why I said that, but I did." She was unmoved by chatter in the Jewish community that Cokie didn't want to marry but preferred to date. "When I dated him, everybody said, 'He's never going to get married.' I said, 'I don't care,' and I married him [in 1957]." He was thirty-four years old, and she was twenty-five.

Renee immediately joined Cokie's family business and worked with him in the shoe department until they sold the business in 1979. Selling shoes gave Renee an expertise that she could apply elsewhere. "I felt like the knowledge that I got from being in business and all the things around it would give me . . . an understanding of life. It really did. For example, when I make an investment, I look at the investment and I say to myself, 'Is that a shoe that belongs in the window, or is that a shoe that I can sell all day Saturday?' In other words, I think about it from the perspective of shoes."

Renee's first foray into the business world occurred at a time when downtown Lexington was glamorous. "In 1957 downtown Lexington was very exciting. And the women came in wearing white gloves; [they] never came down not dressed. Downtown was really wonderful." Hymson's, one of the main downtown stores, had been started in 1938 by Renee's brother-in-law, Maurice. The store had a mystique. It served local folks, but celebrities such as Desi Arnaz and wealthy horsewomen also shopped there. Hymson's fashion shows were elegant affairs in the old Phoenix Hotel, packed with overflow crowds.

Renee's presence in the store may have been overshadowed by that of other family members. Her husband was full of personality, a real showman, and he defied social boundaries and expectations. "When the NAACP [National Association for the Advancement of Colored People] marched, they made a mistake and marched in our store. We couldn't figure it out, [because] we were the ones working for them, so Cokie joined them. And when Cokie joined them, they didn't know what to do. So they

Cokie Hymson in Florida in the 1950s. (Courtesy Renee Hymson.)

left and then they apologized because we were the only store doing what they wanted." Cokie ran the shoe department, while Maurice worked in the clothing department along with his wife, Evelyn. Evelyn, with businesslike demeanor, was singularly focused on manning the enterprise. Where did this leave Renee? She was in the shoe department trying to institute change.

In 1957, according to Renee, the shoe department wasn't so wonderful. It was filled with brown shoes and needed a woman's touch to bring it into full color. "When I came, our department was filled with children's [shoes] and only very basic, and I kept saying, 'You have to have more.

You have to fill it with more fashion, more color,' and I finally talked him [Cokie] into it. He always said that I wanted purple shoes. . . . I wanted more bags, more color, and then I had to have matching bags, and if I could copy them and make them cheaper, all my women [customers] could have a matching bag. That's all I wanted. So we would go to market, and I would find a copy of good bags, 'cause I would first study the expensive bags. And really and truly, my women in those days could have a matching bag starting at $7.98." Renee's passion was that her customers be well served.

She long advocated for her women customers. "Of course, he [Cokie] got glaucoma, and he [would go] to market and say, 'This would sell.' And I'd say, 'That's not terra-cotta, or that's not [whatever color].' He'd say, 'It is!' If I didn't go with him, we would have had orange shoes and bags." She put the customers first and was willing to forgo making a profit if it would have meant giving a woman's needs short shrift. "And then there was one woman that loved our shoes and bags so much, she lived in Winchester. So one time—she wore a size four and a half—I said, 'I don't have anything to fit you today and I'm not going to fit you in the wrong thing.' So the bookkeeper, she got up off the floor when [the customer] was gone and said, 'Mrs. Hymson, is this true? A sale of five purses and no shoes?' It's true. The women, they were just wonderful women. They knew that they could bring it back if it didn't work."

Women came from surrounding central Kentucky communities and even farther afield, riding the train to Lexington from the mountains, to shop at Hymson's. These women were not like Renee, but she related to them nonetheless. "It was a wonderful business. All the mountain women would come by train, and they would come in and look at everything and try [shoes] on. . . . [Then] they'd go down [the street] and turn around and then they'd come back and buy it. I always knew they were coming back. I don't know how, but I always knew it." This Jewish woman from St. Louis had no trouble connecting with the mountain women. "Yeah, I really loved the women. One young girl, twenty-four years old, came in from the mountains, and I said to her, 'Where are your teeth?' And she said, 'The dentist took them all out and I'm going to get new ones.' I said, 'Are you crazy, my God.' I said, 'All right, when you get the teeth, I want you to come here and show me.'"

There are plenty of good stories about Hymson's. It was not just business space but also an intimate place. "The women that came in were such wonderful women," Renee said, "four generations." A friend of Renee's told her children to seek safety in the shoe department with Renee if they ever got separated from her while shopping. "This one friend of mine lived downtown. She always said [to her children], 'If you ever get lost, you can find me at the shoe department at Hymson's.'"

What might seem like quaint business habits were the norm at Hymson's. Suspected thieves were monitored not by cameras or plainclothes security guards but by Yiddish code words. "If somebody came to the store that stole, . . . they'd say, 'Mrs. Goniff is here.' And then it would go all the way back to the shoe department to watch out for Mrs. Goniff. That's Yiddish for thief—*goniff.*" Business competition with other downtown stores didn't preclude cooperation. "Oh, another thing I felt was wonderful: if I didn't have a shoe filler, which you needed for some shoes, I could go across the street to Stewart's shoe department, and he'd give them [to me], or if he was out of something, he'd come over and get it from me. There was actually kindness."

Although Renee's love for the store and the people who frequented it is obvious, she is honest and doesn't hide or camouflage difficulties. There were stressful moments, such as the time she had to direct the babysitter to take her daughter to the hospital emergency room. Renee was at the store one Saturday when "the sitter called, all upset that my daughter [had] slammed her finger in the door and it's hanging by a thread. And this is what a working woman would do. So I said, 'Take a cab to Central Baptist Hospital,' and I met them there."

Renee also had to deal with work and family dynamics that relegated her input to the inconsequential. "We [she and Cokie] didn't always agree, and that was tough because, for example, we sold all the ballet and toe shoes for the ballet company. We had the leotards. I told Cokie I wore leotards all my life in modern dance, [and] you have to get the short sleeves and blah, blah, blah. He said, 'I don't want you in on it.' He turns it over to an employee of ours, and the kid didn't know anything. So we were not in on it together." Another time, Renee and Cokie were purchasing handbags: "I said, 'I can't sell any of these purses in that color,' and he ordered another dozen of them and, of course, they didn't sell. I don't

Renee Hymson and her daughter, modeling clothes for the store. (Courtesy Renee Hymson.)

mean to knock him, but I'm just saying that when a husband and wife are in business, . . . it's [not] that easy. I couldn't understand; when it came to the leotard . . . I always knew the best ones, the best color, everything. So [when] we went to market like that, and then when we bought shoes, . . . he would have the final say about color and style. I don't know how often my opinions won, but that was part of the time. I mean, that would have been considered, I guess, a [male] weakness."

Renee's role in the business was publicly unacknowledged, and she spoke of hurtful events when she felt left out. "I tell you what did bother me, though. My husband ran [an advertisement in the newspaper]. He called it a constitutional ad, and he put all his people's pictures in the ad, and I was never in it. Everybody said, 'Renee, it's okay, we know you're there.' I was never in the ad. He said, 'Well, you don't need to be in a constitutional ad.'"

In Renee's estimation, both Cokie and her parents belittled her. For example, Jenesco, a well-known national shoe company, offered to buy the family shoe store, but only if Renee remained in the business. "I found out that Cokie said to my parents, 'I can't believe Jenesco.' And he and my parents just laughed. I just sat there. When my husband laughed, my parents laughed . . . that really hurt me a lot. I could have laughed with them, and it would have been a joke. It was always a put-down, and that is why I worked so hard for women. Women were not considered. Well, I knew I wasn't [getting credit], but it didn't matter, because I knew what I was doing."

Renee was emboldened to do things other women wouldn't, such as marching herself over to criminal court to collect on bad checks. It was a story Renee wanted to tell: "I would go to criminal court to try to collect bad checks, and it was dangerous really. It was all criminals in there, so I went in, and I had to wait for them to call Hymson's." At court, Renee happened to see the woman who had given her a bad check and confronted her. "I said, 'I'm from Hymson's.' It was the same woman, so I went up to her and I said, 'I want my money.' . . . I said, 'She gave us a check that was bad,'" and [some guy] said, 'So why didn't you know it?' I said, 'Who are you? Who are you? If you ever worked in retail, you would know. You wouldn't ask such a stupid question.' I turned to the judge and I said, 'I really want my money.' So the [woman's] husband had a lawyer—he had been arrested—so the lawyer said, 'Let's just forget about all this.' I said, 'Okay, put him back in the clinker.' And that was all it took. The lawyer said, 'Okay, we pay.' I looked at the man and said, 'Your mother would be ashamed of you.' Anyway, their lawyer went to the bank and I got the money. When I got back to the store, Cokie said, 'I don't know how you got the money.' He said, 'I forgot to give you the important papers that prove that she didn't sign her name right, she signed her husband's name.' And then when I went home, my mother laid [into] me: 'You do not see any other woman in court getting their money.' She was getting hysterical. I said, 'Maybe they're afraid to go, I don't know.' My mother thought it was terrible that I collected the money in criminal court and [that] I would go to the sheriff's office. Because she said, 'Well, your aunt wouldn't do that. I don't know any woman who went to criminal court to collect their money.' She said, 'You should have a lawyer or something.' I didn't have the money to pay a damn lawyer, so I always remember that. That was another generation."

Renee's bold actions and attitudes, so outside the norms of appropriate female behavior in her generation, left her family bewildered and, at times, at odds with her views. "When pantsuits began and I wore a very stylish one to work, my husband didn't know if it was okay," she said. "He didn't know what to think. But that started slow, and then suddenly there were no more white gloves." Men were not the only ones with stale ideas about women. Renee tangled with her mother about women's proper place relative to men when she said she wanted her own daughters to have a college education. "My mother, I was driving, and I said, 'Well, we've got to send them [her daughters] to college and get a job,' and my mother said, 'You can't take a job away from a man.' I said, 'Why not? What if she has to support herself in later years?'" Renee recognized that these differences within the family had to do with shifts in the position of women. "Well, for example, . . . why shouldn't a woman go to court and collect money that's owed to [her]? It had to do with changing times for women."

Through her experiences being a divorced single mom and encountering challenging attitudes at work, Renee developed feminist attitudes. "I know it killed me. It hurt me that women weren't getting their due. It had to do with my life experiences, because I felt so bad for women. They got paid five dollars a day and a man maybe got twenty, and there was no equal thinking involved, and it was not equal thinking in men's minds either." Renee's early career as a model had paid her well, and it gave her perspective on income differentials between men and women. "Well, for example, one time I made a lot of money at fifteen years old, and I taught and worked in different studios as a professional model and taught girls, teenagers in running, say, a fashion show. In those days, . . . the most a woman could make was five dollars a day, [but] I was making five dollars an hour, so it was always amazing to me that the men got away with what they got away with, and the women went along with them."

Renee does not simply spew disenchantment, however disgruntled she might be; rather, she acts. As she entered middle age, she pursued a college degree, even though she was surrounded by much younger students. "I married so young and I had children so young. All I wanted to do was get an education. I went to night school in '69, but it was too hard to go to school and take care of these little babies. And I could hardly keep my eyes open, so I gave up till later in life, when both my kids were in college and I could go during the day and still work in the store. I felt like I was ancient. There was only one other woman my age on campus. I was thirty-eight, and I felt really old because they were all kids. The kids were really nice. They might not have known I was thirty-eight. They were really nice. I would try to do everything, I really did. I tried. I tried to make up because I didn't get to go to college. I had babies [instead]."

After rectifying her own educational deficits, Renee created opportunities for other women. Renee is proud of her labors on behalf of other women, which included helping to start the continuing education program and the Kentucky Women Writers Conference at the University of Kentucky. "Oh, the other thing I did while I was working, I worked really hard for continuing education for women at UK. Every single woman, it seemed like it was such a struggle for them. It was such a strong program. The other thing I worked hard on while I was working was the Women Writers Conference. I was chairman when we had Gloria Steinem [as a guest speaker], and I raised a lot of money."

Renee's involvement with women's causes now lies in the past. Today she is retired, but she still has opinions about women's situations. She has noticed improvements, as well as some circumstances that resist change. Looking at her adult daughters, Renee spots similarities with her own

Renee Hymson today. (Photo by Sarah Jane Sanders.)

life trajectory. One daughter faces financial difficulties even after earning a PhD because, according to Renee, her daughter's educational achievements came too late—after she had raised children and her marriage had dissolved. "No, if she would teach in the public schools, like she did in the beginning, she'd make good money. She didn't want to do that anymore. It was too dangerous. She raised kids, worked, went to school. By the time she got her doctorate, she was too old. She was probably forty-nine. . . . Her [ex-]husband, the dentist, who made all that money—still does— he didn't support the kids. Yeah, he fell in love with his secretary. They have been divorced for like twenty-five years. It's been forever. She could have never existed without our help supporting her children because of the good old boy system in the courts; the lawyers finally collected some money." She blamed the same "good old boy" system for her own child support battles. "And I don't think it's too different today," she said, "because I talk to women who are going through the same thing and, of course, my daughter went through it."

Reminiscent of her own experiences in the store, Renee's daughter's obvious business talents were sometimes mistrusted. "My daughters worked in the store too. And one daughter was excellent in selling. Everybody always loved her. My other daughter was always really brilliant with math. She kept the books for a while. Cokie hired a bookkeeper; it would take him three days [to go] . . . over all of my daughter's figures. 'Nobody could do it in three hours,' [he claimed], . . . 'cause see, my daughter could do it in three hours, and he didn't trust it. He would go over it like a crazy man."

Along with tales of stasis, though, Renee recognizes some positive developments. For instance, her efforts to provide continuing education at the University of Kentucky paid off. "UK did give us money. . . . To this day, it [the continuing education program] is still there, and it is a very big thing."

The similarities between Renee and Manar and Sawsan are palpable, although they may become visible only when one tends to their words. Make no mistake: their most substantial commonality is that their stories have been hidden. Renee was a working mother before the very concept had taken hold. Today, for better or worse, it is the norm. But contemporary mothering archetypes overlook Muslim women like Sawsan and Manar, whose day-to-day lives resemble those of other middle-class women, despite their differences and distance from these others.

ARCHETYPAL AND
DISTANT FIGURES

HOW DOES ONE WRITE ABOUT WOMEN who have long since died—women who, if alive, would be well over a hundred years old and whose sons, who are relaying their stories, are themselves old men? In this chapter, ninety-one-year-old Mike Rowady talks about his Lebanese mother, Rose Rowady, who passed away in the late 1970s. Ninety-three-year-old Franklin Moosnick describes his Jewish mother (my grandmother), Rose Moosnick, who died some forty-six years ago (my uncle Franklin has also passed away since our interviews). The two Roses are distant figures evoked by men reminiscing about their mothers late in their own lives.

Much could be written on how sons talk about their mothers, especially men who are presumably at nostalgic moments in their own lives. A sort of romance exists between Mike and Franklin and their mothers; they offer mostly glowing stories of women who were masters of the home and beyond. Maternal heroines are presented. Franklin, for instance, spoke of his mother's cooking: "She was a very good cook and, actually, spoiled me for most of the other ladies' cooking because it was always delicious, well seasoned. She used lots of spices and it wasn't just bland cooking."

Certainly, there is more to these women's stories than cooking. My grandmother, "Mama Rose," had a presence in our home even though she died when I was just a baby. My father regularly called to mind her memory. I would listen to my father credit Mama Rose for having the foresight to purchase the antiques that graced our living room, before they were either fashionable or valuable. My mother, in the kitchen lighting a cigarette, would have a counterresponse: "That woman was too much. She was overbearing." My sister likes to say, "Mom never got over her." No doubt, the story told depends on one's vantage point, recognizing that all relationships are unique.

The intention of this chapter is to tell stories that might otherwise be forgotten because these women's imprints have been left mainly on their family members, most deeply on the eldest family members. But both the acknowledged and the unacknowledged marks that Rose and Rose made mirror the marks left by countless Arab and Jewish women in the past. Rose and Rose are archetypes representing others like them—immigrant mothers determined to see that their children became financially and socially successful. It is an uncommon occasion to recognize women who might otherwise dissolve into family lore and to appreciate that their stories resonate with those of countless women. Accordingly, unlike in previous chapters, I do not parcel out their stories separately but weave them together as like and merging tales (with their own particular nuances), illustrating the closeness of their accounts.

Promoting an appreciation for women who died years ago, and linking past lives to current ones, counters a cultural practice that treats earlier lives as remote and isolated from contemporary contexts. It's easy to think that the present has no relationship to the past when the larger cultural situation in which Rose and Rose mothered and Mike and Franklin spent their childhoods is so distant. In the early twentieth century, communication was slow compared to today's standards. People wrote letters to convey messages. "Communication in the family in those days was by letter," said Franklin. "Gee, to pick up the phone, it was only to announce that somebody had died." Consumer culture had not taken hold, and ready-made goods were not in abundant supply. Clothes were still handmade, and processed foods had yet to be developed. Mike remembered, "They made their own stuff. They spun their own cloth. It was what people did." According to their sons, the two Roses were adept at both the sewing machine and the stove—skills that are making a comeback today among those who call for a return to local foods and goods. Rose and Rose used their skills to survive during economically challenging times (the Great

Depression) in small-town Kentucky, turning their talents to economic advantage. They managed life for their families before middle-class suburban life existed.

These women laid foundations for future lives. They, like so many women, focused not on themselves but on the possibilities for and prospects of their progeny. Their efforts worked. While adversity may have defined much of the two Roses' stories, achievement marks later generations.

Rose Rowady arrived in Kentucky somewhere around 1909. Her son, Mike, is a native son and longtime resident of the state. He's active and ensconced in Winchester, Kentucky, a small community of approximately 16,000 people. Everywhere he goes—properly dressed—he's known and recognized. He speaks his mind, and he's regularly asked to speak about Winchester's past—both formally at the local historical society and informally at the local coffee shop. He doesn't mind telling you that so-and-so had family in the KKK or that a person walking by comes from "society." Professional and social success characterizes him, as it does members of his family.

Likewise, Franklin Moosnick was well positioned socially, professionally, and economically. Through his medical career, he touched countless people in central Kentucky. And he, along with his wife, Marilyn (who has also died since the interviews), engaged in community activities, making their name locally recognizable.

But behind all the accolades and achievements are men with immigrant roots who came from humble beginnings. Their mothers symbolize their trajectory from hardship to accomplishment. Rose and Rose lived to see their adult children thrive, and as a result, they too enjoyed upper mobility. They were survivors. *Survivor* is a word that Mike uses a lot when talking about his mother. "She needed to get these kids educated somewhere, and she lived to see it happen. Like Joe, who was the chicken fighting king out here and one of the most interesting people. He knew her. He'd shake his head every once in a while [and say], 'How in the hell she did it I don't know, to survive that Depression.'"

Mike and Franklin both noted moments when they and their widowed mothers appreciated having economic stability. A new dress or lack thereof was emblematic for Rose Moosnick. Franklin recalled, "Through

Mike Rowady. (Photo by Sarah Jane Sanders.)

Rose Rowady and her family, after achieving financial success. (Courtesy Mike Rowady.)

the years on High Holy Days, when we would go to synagogue, and whether it was in Poughkeepsie or Lexington, she would take her black dress and put a little lace around the collar or make a belt or do something to it, lengthen it, shorten it, according to the style. It was always the same dress, but it looked different. And I said to her once, 'Here it is Rosh Hashanah this weekend, and have you gotten a new dress yet? It was always so important to you to have a new dress or fix up your old one or something.' And she said, 'Well, when we couldn't afford it, it was very important to have a new dress, and when you could afford it, it wasn't so important anymore.'"

Likewise, Rose Rowady had to adjust to her newfound financial security once Mike started making money as a lawyer. "One of the last discussions I had with her: She had property down there for rent, and Main Street had begun to die down. After we had finally got her out of the store, we'd rent to people, and then so-and-so didn't pay the rent. I was starting to do pretty well in the mid-sixties, and so one day I had a discussion with her. . . . She called up [concerned about the unpaid rent] and I said, 'Look, Mom, I'm busy. I don't have time to fool with that, but

Rose Moosnick wearing her best dress. (Courtesy Moosnick family.)

I'll make you one promise: if I eat, you do too. Don't call me again about this.' She never did."

ROSE ROWADY AND ROSE MOOSNICK
WINCHESTER AND VERSAILLES, KENTUCKY

Relaxing their efforts to achieve economic security must have felt far removed from their initial forays to Kentucky. Rose Rowady hailed from a mountainous community near Palestine, an area noted for its fresh fruits and hand-strung goods. "Well, she was born in a mountain six miles from Palestine," said Mike. "Those people weren't dumb. Where they lived— I saw some literature—it's very hot around there, but this is very high elevation—8,000, 9,000 feet up there—so it's a place where people who have money go in the summertime. But they [Rose's family] lived there year-round and had their own type of crops and their own animals, goats and stuff like that, that they raised, especially grapes and grape vineries. . . . They would dry apricots and peaches, and if you get any from over there, it's very good, high-quality stuff, tastes good."

Despite being born in Boston, Rose Moosnick was a New Yorker, and she came from an educated background. "They [Rose's family] were Pearlmans. They were Blooms," said Franklin. "There was a group in Boston where my mother was born actually. I think when their family came over they went to Boston because they already had family there named Brown, and that's all I know about them. I don't know where they were from, but I presume they were from Poland, Lithuania, one of the Baltic states there. And her family, at least her mother, came from, I think, fairly well-educated, well-off kind of people. I say that because she would refer to other people in Yiddish [as] *orem*, like peasants: 'Look at so-and-so; they have this nice store just like *orem.*'"

Mike's mother also came from some wealth. "She was brought up with a little elegance, with servants. They sent a servant with her to go to school. . . . It was a boarding school, [and] the servant stayed with her and brought her back."

Much about their early lives has been lost, even simple details like the years they were born. That's not unexpected, in Mike's estimation, because women of his mother's generation and culture were not formally documented. "He [Mike's maternal grandfather] made grapes, and he'd dry the grapes and take a caravan into Egypt because it wasn't too far, and [he'd] sell these raisins down there. There was a little river down there, and while they were in the river, a bag of the raisins broke and fell in the river, and that's when Mama was born, that was her birthday: when the raisins fell in the river. They didn't keep what year it was. Kept only the men's."

Both Mike and Franklin felt compelled to highlight their mothers' fine educational pedigrees. Maybe they did so to compensate for their mothers' lack of recognition in the past, or maybe they did so to separate their mothers from the wave of immigrants who flocked to urban locales in this country and were widely seen as dirty and uncouth. Either way, it's clear that these women were like many others around them, and their sophistication may have been overshadowed by their immigrant or daughter-of-immigrant status.

And like so many others, the two Roses knew work, not leisure. In 1909 Rose Rowady and her brother left Lebanon and arrived in New York Harbor, following a route taken earlier by their other brothers and sisters. Rose avoided the normal Ellis Island registration procedures and instead jumped into a boat managed by her sister and her sister's husband. "When they [Rose and her brother] got to New York, there were so many people getting off at Ellis Island that if you knew anybody, they'd hire a boat, and she never did go through the registration. They just picked her up in a boat and took her." Once in the States, Rose helped a brother peddle fine linens and rugs in Pennsylvania, North Carolina, and Kentucky. She was his interpreter. "She was working there in New York and then over to Wilkes-Barre. They kind of moved around. He [Rose's brother] was traveling and selling oriental rugs and tapestries and handwork, and she could even make this stuff, so he took her around and down to maybe Fayetteville, North Carolina. And then [they were] traveling up through here [Kentucky], selling stuff to the horse people that had those farms and [bought] big fine rugs and things. . . . My uncle Nick had her going around with him primarily because she could speak and write in English, and she was a help to him, making it easier. Although he spoke rather well, she was good."

Rose Moosnick, meanwhile, spent her life in New York City. Her own mother died in childbirth, so Rose was raised by a stepmother among her stepsisters and stepbrothers. Franklin caught glimpses of his mother's former urban life on the regular trips to New York that he took with her and his brother. "We would go to New York like every three years for Mother to visit her stepmother and her stepsisters, 'cause everybody had the same father but different mothers, because the women would sicken and die in childbirth. So we'd go see Aunt Eddie, Aunt Sarah, Grandma, and then there were a lot of cousins that we would see." Before Rose moved to Versailles, Kentucky, with her own family, she worked in the millinery section of Macy's department store. "She had an eye for style. She'd take a hat and she would decorate it or clip it."

How is it that both Roses ended up in Kentucky? They followed the lead set by men—whether husbands, brothers, or others. Rose Rowady was peddling in central Kentucky when her brother heard of a man who needed a wife. "They said, 'You want a woman, we've got one. She belongs to your church. She looks like you; she comes from your same ethnic background.' We're all Phoenicians together from a thousand years, so there it is." Meanwhile, Rose Pearlman (at the time) was matched with Lazarus Moosnick, a Lithuanian peddler who moved to New York after his store in Meridian, Mississippi, was ruined in floods. "While his store was being refurbished, he went to New York to visit his family, and while there—in those days, all marriages were an arranged marriage. 'I think you would be great with her or she would be great with you,' and that was all it took. There was no real romancing. So he met my mother and they got married," said Franklin.

The places they chose to raise their families followed economic and familial connections. Rose Rowady and her husband, Alex—along with some extended family, the Thomases—settled in Winchester. Rose Moosnick started her family in Poughkeepsie, New York; this was a compromise because her husband didn't care for the city, and she was not ready to extricate herself from New York. Franklin's father talked about going back to Mississippi, he recalled, but "for a girl who had lived all her life in New York, you can imagine her saying, 'Mississippi?' But my father didn't like the city, and so they compromised on Poughkeepsie, which, at that time, was [considered] way upstate." At the urging of Lazarus's brother Phillip, who lived in Nicholasville, Kentucky, and in the face of Lazarus's dissatisfaction with working for someone else, the family moved to Kentucky in 1924, pouring all their savings into a store in Versailles. "He [Franklin's father] was always by himself, and then when we were in Poughkeepsie, he peddled for a while in Dutchess County. Then he went to work for someone who had a clothing store, and he didn't like the supervision. We came to Nicholasville and we lived with Uncle Phillip for about six months maybe, until my father could look around and find a location for a store. And by that time, our savings were pretty well dissipated and we had very little money. I think we started the store with something like $400 that we had saved up."

Both Roses were determined and pragmatic women focused on the progress of their families, so they didn't harp on the fact that they weren't living among other Jews or Arabs in Kentucky. They were strong, strong women—or so I heard. New York City–bred Rose Moosnick adapted to Versailles, Kentucky. "I think once she took up roots in Versailles, I think she was really happy with it," said Franklin. "She was very pragmatic about things. I think wherever she went, she tried to make a life for herself wherever she was. I think when she was in Versailles, after just a period, she accepted what it was and made her life there and didn't second-guess it."

Physically small women, they stood firm nonetheless. Mike depicted his mother as follows: "She was small and slender. I don't guess she ever weighed 120 in her life, 'cause she just didn't eat a lot. Well, she was an inscrutable person. There was something about her. I never saw anybody—she was solid steel. She had no conception of fear. Now, if anybody came up that challenged us children, they had to deal with her. She had a way to make people know. When it came to whatever she was doing, [she was a] fearless and unyielding and powerful woman, and you never knew it—except people who knew her knew it. She was always messy—never dirty, but her clothes were in a shambles. But when she dressed up, she looked grand. She had noble features and high cheekbones. You would have liked her."

Rose and Rose needed a touch of nobility and strength, because marriage did not bring them a life free of work—quite the contrary. These women were connected to their sewing machines and cooking stoves both at home and in the store. It's almost as though these appliances were

Rose Rowady as a young woman (left) and later in life (right). (Courtesy Mike Rowady.)

appendages of Rose Rowady. "She had a sewing machine and a cooking stove back there and was running, doing all that back there by herself," said Mike. Lines between home and work blurred. Both families lived behind or above their stores, and business overlapped with home life. Rose Rowady's family ran a grocery and fruit market that, according to Mike, was a less than desirable business. "Selling fruit and that kind of stuff, and we'd have fish imported from Baltimore and oysters in season. You didn't have refrigeration. I hated that store. I hated it with a passion. I was embarrassed. It seemed like it was dirty. There were rats around there, but there were rats around everywhere in those days."

In Rose Moosnick's case, the J. L. Moosnick Store sold dry goods. Initially, it was tucked away in a small space on Court Street; only years later did the store make it to Main Street. "The store was not that big," Franklin recalled. "The storefront was maybe twenty-five or twenty feet wide and thirty feet deep, something like that." The small store corresponded to the family's small living quarters. "We lived behind it [the store]. There were two or three steps up. Everything is on a hill there, and the store was on Court Street level. You walked in from the street and it was level. And then the back side of it was elevated—three steps, something like—and we lived behind the store. There was a kitchen in the back and another room in between the store, and there was a door that would close, and so we lived there. We slept all in one room and [had] the kitchen in back, and we lived there." The living quarters might have been small, but Rose Moosnick made certain they were presentable. "My mother had the place—she made curtains and drapes. It was to the point that [when] people came to see us occasionally they were shocked at how lovely it was. She made an attractive, lovely home out of these three rooms."

These were skilled women, capable and entrepreneurial at home and elsewhere. Rose Rowady came from a line of tough women: carved into Mike's memory are images of his maternal grandmother smoking a pipe she had brought from Lebanon and of his aunt Amelia, who was more assertive than even New Yorkers. Mike's maternal grandmother was the only grandparent he knew. "She smoked a *nargeela,* which is a pipe, and [she] brought it here with her." This pipe-smoking grandmother produced three daughters, each of whom was implacable. "All those three girls were just excellent at doing well. I think my aunt Amelia, she was the toughest one, and she met all those rich people in New York and designed clothes for them. She was the darnedest and went to work in the garment industry. And she'd go and try to buy something, and the guy would say no, and she'd keep hammering down and finally he'd say, 'Lady, you give me a headache.' She'd say, 'Take an aspirin.' We'd walk across Seventh Avenue, cars coming, and I'd say, 'Auntie, we're going to get killed.' 'They'll wait. They'll wait.' She was tough." Mike's mother, though not as tough as her sister, still had the skills and the will to ensure that her family did not perish. "She was making clothes, growing a garden, eating the fruit we couldn't sell, rotten fruit. And I guess that's why I'm alive, 'cause we ate all these fruits and drank olive oil. I think people [who] eat a lot of fruit and use olive oil probably never get cancer."

The two Roses' sewing and cooking skills made an impression on their sons and provide an observable contrast to today's domestic practices focused on quick results. Franklin recalled, "She was a very good cook, as a matter of fact. She was willing to experiment [with] what you would call soul food. When she made chicken soup, she would cook the chicken long enough to get the chicken flavor in the soup, and she would take it out real quick and then put it in the oven and broil it, and we would have broiled chicken. . . . And she baked and made cakes and all those things on a regular basis." So scrumptious was Rose Rowady's food that Mike's Jewish friend lamented that his kosher practices kept him from sampling her fine baked goods. "But God, she could make delicate things," marveled Mike. "I told you that Arthur Herman said that he wished to hell he had violated the law and tasted some of the things she cooked." Likewise, the two men recalled the laborious skill required to expertly produce clothing at home. Mike called his mother "the best designer who made clothes out of flour sacks. She could sew. Best suit I had, she made, and I paid $3,000 for a tailored suit when I had money." Franklin, too, admired his mother, who could not only sew but also assemble stylish garb. "She was a genius with the sewing machine. She had an eye for style and was able to—well, when we were kids, for instance, she would take a piece of newspaper and hold it up to you and mark it and cut it and lay the piece of paper on the fabric and cut it and sew it and make a suit or a pair of pants or a blouse."

Old-country remedies, not Western approaches, are what Rose Rowady relied on when it came to curing her ailing children. "My mother was a person of numerous talents," said Mike, "and one of them was her remedies for colds." She was also successful curing more complex problems. "So, her fifth and sixth children were born terribly bowlegged. It was a joke around town that you could roll a round watermelon between their legs (since we were selling fruit) and not touch the sides. But they had this group of orthopedic people for children who were crippled or deformed. My mother took my brother and my sister up to see them, and they said, 'Well, we'll have to break the legs' and all that. She said, 'No, no thank you.' I can remember her doing this every day for hours: rubbing their legs with olive oil, to push it in. And I don't know whether that had anything to do with it, but with time, they got five or six years older, and their legs were straight. She got rid of it. She did that for hours. She'd be pushing on their legs."

The Roses' domestic skills were also employed to generate income. They were "working" women (even if they were not recognized as such), and their daily lives revolved around not just the home but also the family business. In the store, Rose Moosnick, a skilled saleswoman, reconfigured

merchandise to suit her customers. "Mother would take a pair of pants—
you didn't have every size and every length—so she would lengthen or
shorten or put false cuffs on them, and put a little fold . . . if they were too
big in the waist." Rose Moosnick also took the bus to Louisville and Cincinnati, making buying trips for the store and for specific customers. "On
more expensive dresses, she would buy them with a particular person
in mind that she thought she could sell it to. And when she came back,
she would call them up and say, 'I saw a dress that reminded me of you
and I want you to come in and try it on and see.' And they would come
in and usually buy whatever she had picked out for them. Or they might
say something to her about having to go to a family reunion or a wedding
and [say], 'I need a dress that I can wear after, nothing too fancy.' So when
she made her next trip, she would look for that type of thing." She'd drag
the goods back with her on the bus to Versailles, bribing the bus drivers
to let her carry her purchases to avoid the shipping costs. Meanwhile,
her husband and sons would be waiting at the bus stop to meet her. "The
bus station was on Main Street. You'd go up Main Street from the store,
turn left, and maybe half a dozen storefronts' distance. And when the bus
was due, Monroe [Franklin's brother] and I would get our wagons and go
around there. Dress boxes were long, deep, and wide, and great big boxes
loaded with fabrics, they would weigh a ton. They [his parents] would get
[the boxes] off and tip the drivers for helping her put them on, and we
would whip around the corner to the store. But when it comes to making
a living, not having to pay freight charges or delivery charges and so on
was a big piece of money saved, and for three or four dollars, which was
the bus fare in those days, you could save three, four, or five times that
much in freight charges."

Tucked away in these narratives is the intimation that these women
were more adroit than their husbands in the trading realm. Franklin
never said so, but Mama Rose's sister, Sarah, did. My outspoken great-
aunt Sarah, on her regular visits to Kentucky from New York, would
narrate the family story differently from my father and uncle. She often
complained that she never understood why Laz, my grandfather, ever
took Mama Rose away from New York. Sarah asserted that Mama Rose
was the mastermind behind the business, not Laz. "Laz never would have
made it if it weren't for Rose," was Aunt Sarah's refrain.

Mike, meanwhile, spoke lovingly of his father, who was a gentle man but not a talented entrepreneur. "My father wasn't aggressive. New merchandise came, chain stores came. They were buying in quantities and selling cheaper, and he . . . was selling fancy merchandise. It troubled him that people would buy apples with knots, holes, and worms, and he was selling this beautiful stuff. He couldn't understand that, and he couldn't adjust to it." Mike said point-blank that his mother had a steadfastness that escaped his father. "I don't think he [Mike's father] was afraid of anything, but he should have been the momma and she should have been the papa. She was pushing to get ahead and [was] behind us all the time. He never pushed us because he knew that Mom was doing it, and he was satisfied with the results and [knew] that we weren't in any real trouble. She wasn't what you'd call cruel or anything like that. She told us that we were in this mess and we're not going anywhere."

For Mike, one story stands out that epitomizes his mother's assertiveness and his father's mild temperament. "I always thought that she invented the sit-down tactic. I remember Happy Chandler was inaugurated [governor] in December of 1935. One of the first things he did, there was a license tax to sell cigarettes in the retail stores that was payable to the state: twenty-five dollars. Twenty-five dollars was a lot then. It only cost thirty-nine dollars to go to the University of Kentucky, [and] that included your tickets to ball games, football and basketball. So the cigarette tax was one of the first things repealed, and all the merchants were notified to go to the county clerk's office to get a refund. Well, my father went there day after day, and the county clerk, Mr. Linville Jackson, was always too busy. 'Come back another day,' [he'd say]. We were living upstairs, and my mother came down all dressed up, and my father said, 'Where are you going, Rosie?' And she said, 'I'm going up to get the refund for the tax.' He says, 'That's men's work. They won't pay any attention to you.' She said, 'Well, you've tried and failed, and I'm going to try myself.' So she goes and she's gone about two hours. Finally, [she] came back. 'Did you get it?' 'Yeah, here it is.' 'Well, how did you get it?' 'Well, Mr. Jackson said, "I'm busy. Come back some other day."' She said, 'Well, I'm not,' and sat down, took a chair right in front and she sat there about two hours, and finally he wrote the check."

Rose Rowady had no intention of forgoing twenty-five dollars because, to a certain extent, economic hardship had become a steady companion for Mike's family, especially after his father's health deteriorated. "He was ill from '24 'cause they took him here at this hospital, operated on him for gallstones, and it was in April. I remember it very well. They left him there at the window and he got cold. . . . He started coughing, and he ruptured the whole thing. They wanted to redo it, and we didn't have the money. Mama would make these trusses for him out of burlap bags. He wore them until he died [twelve years later]." His father's illness set the family back for numerous reasons. For one thing, the other Lebanese in Winchester, their extended family, left to pursue opportunities in the Detroit area, whereas Mike's family could not leave because of his father's ill health. "My uncle George Thomas couldn't read or write, but Papa said he could count. He was always making money. He was daring, and his children are that way, and all well educated, two or three PhDs and lawyers. And all of them made just enormous amounts of money in Michigan, and Papa wouldn't go. I don't think he could have gone. He was sick at that time, when they pulled up [and left] in '25 or so."

The Rowadys' environment, where Mike and his family dwelled and traded, was a difficult one. "There was a drugstore three doors down, and I have to mention that because after that, . . . it became a brothel. Anyway, after it morphed into this, nice guys would go up and beat these women. You'd hear screaming. They were upstairs. They used to walk the street morning to night and wear these dresses with the long front till the factories came. And a lot of those girls came out of the mountains. When they got fourteen, fifteen years old, they were kicked out [of their homes and told] to go find yourself something to do." Rose Rowady's trials were more pronounced than Rose Moosnick's because her husband died when Mike was sixteen, leaving her alone to support seven children in a tough neighborhood filled with brothels, prostitutes, gamblers, and bootleggers.

Yet both Roses knew difficult times. They lacked the economic or educational advancement their children and grandchildren now enjoy, and they were isolated in their small towns, with few others like them. They were not always sure they were welcome in their communities. Rose and Rose were raising their families in the 1920s, when the Ku Klux Klan was on the ascendency in small-town Kentucky. Klan members were not distant figures; they were neighbors or maybe even playmates. Franklin recalled, "In Versailles I remember one thing. Nowadays they call it a play date, but I went over after school with one of my buddies to his house to play. I was old enough. He and I played pretty nice, and then all of a sudden on his back porch hammered into the wall [I saw] nails driven in that made KKK. I didn't know that about him, but my feelings toward him became kind of lukewarm after that, for no reason other than seeing that. It wasn't anything he said or did, but you knew that his attitudes had to be related to that."

Rose and Rose pushed ahead in their uncertain social milieus, where, from time to time, people disparaged their children. Even in their nineties, Franklin and Mike vividly recalled some of their uncomfortable encounters. Franklin was taunted on the playground in Nicholasville—something he had not experienced in Poughkeepsie. "Well, in Nicholasville I remember two things particularly. One of them was the first day I went to school. We got out at like ten o'clock for recess, and on the playground all these kids started taunting me, calling me a 'dirty Jew' and 'Christ killer.' I didn't know what the hell they were talking about, 'cause coming from Poughkeepsie, I had never heard of anything like that. I didn't know what they were talking about really."

Mike, even more so than Franklin, talked about unjust treatment at school—and not just from the kids. Some of the teachers did not necessarily want to see a "garlic eater" excel. "I had a chemistry course. Nice man [the teacher], popular. There was . . . a five-day test. I didn't think anything about it. It was an easy course for me. . . . On the fourth day he announced to the class that I had led the class for three straight days, and he knew I wasn't that smart, knew that I was cheating. But he wasn't able to detect it, so to prevent me from doing that (and all those rich people were in there, 'cause during the Depression, they weren't sending them away to school, they were going to the Winchester high school), so he moved me up [front] and my grade dropped, I guess under the pressure. He got up the next day and announced that [that] proved I was cheating. I should have knocked the crap out of him, but you know, I was taught to never attack them. Last time I saw that man [was] just before he died; he was in his eighties. We were in Dawhares [a Lebanese-owned department store], and I was getting something. He was getting a suit fixed, and I heard him say—he wanted me to hear it, I guess, by way of apology—that 'one of the most uncomfortable things for a teacher is to have a student who knew more than he did.' I heard him say that. He knew that I had not forgotten it. I know he knew it, but I'm not going to feel vindicated over it, but it hurt. I had another teacher. I was a troublemaker, I cannot deny that I really was, saying funny things and disruptive. And this teacher was a math teacher and [she] said, 'No wisecracks from the garlic eaters.' See, she thought I was Italian, so, 'No wisecracks from the garlic eaters.'"

Nuanced differences are apparent in the Roses' reaction to the Klan and the mistreatment of their children. They both, no doubt, forged ahead, aiming for their families to overcome social and class barriers. Rose Rowady was aware of the Klan's presence, and, according to Mike, his father was even invited to participate in a KKK rally—an offer he declined. Curiously, Mike portrayed his mother as almost too busy to give too much weight to others' actions or to focus on it overtly. He grasped that his mother did not react to jeering the same way he did. "She didn't let it bother her. She's a confident person. I don't know, kind of a rock of ages person. Let them think what the heck they wanted to; she was just there, and she had her obligations. She needed to get these kids educated somewhere, and she lived to see it happen. Mama was struggling to keep us going all the time, never was discouraged, and never felt like I did. Her attitude was if they didn't like me, the hell with them."

Racial and ethnic difficulties were not analyzed or discussed at length, but Rose and Lazarus Moosnick recognized their existence. "They [Franklin's parents] just [said], 'That's just the way it is.' What else are you going to say? You aren't going to change it. And the other thing in Nicholasville that I remember is during the summer that we were there—we came in the late spring and we left around Thanksgiving time—and during the summer there was a Ku Klux Klan parade with horses all covered with white robes and people with the masks and the white robes parading down the street. I remember I didn't understand what was going on. I sensed that my parents were just uptight, and so I knew that whatever it was, it was something to be afraid of." The fear that permeated Franklin's rendering was not present in Mike's version.

In small-town Kentucky, it might have been fear that propelled Rose Moosnick to cling to her Jewish heritage, whereas Rose Rowady did not insist that her children marry Catholics or other Lebanese. Not surpris-

Franklin and Marilyn's wedding photo, with Rose Moosnick in the center and Monroe and Sonia Moosnick to the left. (Courtesy Moosnick family.)

ingly, Mike did not marry a Lebanese woman, and his Arab American identity has become diluted. In contrast, ethnicity and religion—in this case, being Jewish—mattered in Franklin's family. Rose Moosnick made sure they kept kosher, even though they were virtually the only Jewish family in town and had to go elsewhere to get kosher meats. "Well, we were different, in a sense," said Franklin. Moosnick's was the only store, for instance, that closed on the High Holidays. "And we were the only family that people had ever heard of who kept kosher at home." Naturally, it was important to Rose Moosnick that her boys marry Jewish women, so it's not surprising that Franklin and Monroe married late—at ages forty and thirty-eight, respectively—because of the pressure to marry Jews in a world without many Jewish prospects. "Well, they [Franklin's parents] expected us to be strongly identified with Jews. When we were old enough to date, you didn't go out with anybody—or we might go out with somebody once, but you never went out with them twice—unless they were Jewish, as a real date. After I came back to town after World War II and was living in Lexington and was dating, I would date Jewish girls, [but] I would date non-Jewish girls too. [If] I was dating one girl, a non-Jewish girl, with any frequency, they would say something to me about the fact: 'Are you sure you're not getting too involved there that you can't back out?'"

Although Franklin married outside of the religion, his wife readily converted to Judaism and raised their children to be Jewish, in part because she had no familial ties. "Marilyn was an orphan. And quite honestly, the fact that she was an orphan was probably one of the reasons why I was able to marry her. There were no home objections, and she was able to convert totally without any baggage hanging behind her." At forty years old, Franklin was still concerned about meeting his widowed mother's marital expectations for him.

Clinging to their identity was one response to isolation. Being civic oriented was another. Rose and Laz Moosnick willed the family to be civic and community minded, unlike other Jews who resided in the area. "There were Jews, but none of them were what you call practicing Jews," said Franklin. "They were Jews in name. There was a store directly across from where we were on Main Street. And they were there a number of years. I never knew them, but my parents did, and they liked them just in passing. They weren't close friends or anything. Our family was the first one that was really integrated into the community. Now, the other store was just a merchant, [and the proprietors] had no friends that I know of in the community, just acquaintances." Outfitting their customers well was a priority for Rose and Laz. "They knew every customer, and they knew all the children, and they would not . . . do anything that would be to the customer's detriment. They would always try to make sure the customer [was satisfied]. Like a lot of times the customer would [choose one] shirt, and my father would say to them, 'That's not the shirt for you. You really would do better with this shirt.' From . . . my father's point of view, he was putting himself in the place of the customer and knew what would suit them best and their lifestyle best, and maybe suit their parents the best, and that happened all the time." Being good merchants translated into being good community members for Laz and Rose.

Mike's mother, in contrast, shunned community engagement, pre-

Rose and Lazarus Moosnick. (Courtesy Moosnick family.)

ferring to keep to herself and focus on raising and educating her seven children. "I felt like she was aloof. She was so bound up in that family and seeing us get out of that prison [that] . . . Thomas Wolfe said, 'Which of us is not forever prison pent, which of us is not forever a stranger and alone.' She thought . . . we had to get out of there. That was her whole desire."

The two Roses chose different ways to manage their lives in small-town Kentucky. Yet they were alike: two women who were unaware of boundaries and would not accept the word *no*. Mike told a story that typified his mother's willfulness: Rose Rowady managed to get her daughter into the University of Kentucky, even after she had been rejected. "I remember when my sister was trying to go to the University of Kentucky. She met Dean Holmes and all that, [and] they said [they didn't have a place for her], even though she had really good grades in school. So then she was going to [go to] Fugazzi [a secretarial and business school for women], and Mama went with her. . . . As they are walking in Lexington, heading for Fugazzi, Mama says, 'Let's go back to the university.' And Julia said, 'Oh, it won't do any good,' [but Mama] says, 'We're going anyway.' And while she was talking to Dean Holmes, there was a girl from Pikeville who they said they had a place for, [but she] said she couldn't come, and [Julia] got that spot. But Mama was tenacious. She was unyielding."

Life transitions occurred in both families. The stores went out of business as the children became adults and professionals, as was supposed to happen in Franklin's rendering. "It's the usual story: almost all of the people whose parents [were] in business, unless the business was a major business, a big enough store and that kind of thing, all looked for their children to become professional people, teachers. But I don't think [my parents] ever had any intention for us to continue the store."

In both cases, the sons eventually took over parts of their mothers' lives, assuming responsibilities and making choices and decisions for them. But this doesn't mean that their mothers' willfulness declined. They may not have been working in their businesses, but other things consumed them. Rose Rowady became a landlord, and Rose Moosnick periodically worked at another Jewish-owned store in Lexington. She was an accomplished saleswoman who was unwilling to let a woman leave the store with just one item. As Franklin recalled, she had trouble writing up sales slips, which was something she was not acquainted with. "But she was such a good salesperson," he said. "She wasn't content with selling a dress; you had to buy underwear, you had to buy a scarf, and you had to buy a belt. She was just a fantastic salesperson, so Maurice [the store owner] had somebody else follow her around and write up her sales slips and let her do the selling."

Rose and Rose responded to changing times. Rose Moosnick filled her life with friends and cooked for neighbors and renters after she was widowed and was no longer tied to the store. "She had a number of friends and ultimately a number of groups. But at that time, she was in her late fifties, early sixties. She made a life for herself here in Lexington. She had a number of friends." Rose Rowady got a television and learned about basketball and football. As Mike said, "She learned pretty fast, too, and when television came, she learned about basketball and football and things like that. She was never a person interested in politics, [but] she was a profound Democrat. She was always talking about mean Republicans. I'm getting teary about this thing."

Old habits continued, and boundaries remained elusive to the Roses. Mama Rose's insistence that she inspect my brother's report cards went unappreciated by my mother, who had a strong sense that her son's grades were a private matter. Rose Rowady managed to get into a University of Kentucky football game without a ticket. Mike and his wife were attending the football game while Rose did some shopping downtown, and they had arranged to meet later. Mike remembered, "I think [it was] the last time Kentucky played Georgia Tech, [when] the football team still played [at] Stoll Field. . . . [Mama] was going to go shopping at Wolf Wiles and all those other stores downtown. We were going to meet her at the Phoenix Hotel after the game. . . . [Then], here comes Mama, and I said, 'Who gets in the football game?' I said, 'How did you get in?' 'I walked through the door.' She just [went] right through. The guard saw this old woman. That's the kind of person she was. . . . We were about halfway up the stadium, and she found us [in], what, 20,000 people in those days. I'll never forget: we were ahead in the first half and lost in the second. She said, 'What kind of game is that? They get up there in a pile, whisper to each other, and then they jump on each other.' Nothing would stop her. Whenever she decided to do something, there wasn't any travail. She just did it. She never felt inferior to anybody. Nobody made her feel bad."

Concluding Reflections

When we spoke, many years had passed since their mothers died, and evidence of their own mortality was ever present. Both Mike and Franklin were pensive about their mothers and recognized the contributions the Roses had made to their own successes. Mike likes to say that he never would have made it without his mother. The Roses were strong, forceful women, even long after their child-rearing days were over. Rose Rowady died with a mop in her hands and canned beans on her counter. She was never tired, never hungry—so pronounces Mike. Mike took Rose to visit Thomas Jefferson's estate, Monticello, and while touring the home, he lost sight of her. She just disappeared, and he nearly panicked. But when he found her, there she sat in the garden next to the fig trees, peeling and eating figs. "They'll arrest you," Mike yelled at his mother. "I'm too old," was her response. She simply preferred to rest among the fruit trees, reminiscent of her Lebanese home.

Mama Rose could never be fully disconnected from her New York roots. She had an urban personality and was fixed on getting and making her way, even in a nonurban setting. In our family lore, no other family character has so much presence in our lives so long after her death. My cousin chuckled recently at the memory of Mama Rose feigning disbelief, almost to the point of fainting, at the price of an antique she was interested in. She would invariably leave the shop with the piece and a smirk, having convinced the clerk to lower his price to meet her ideal.

Rose and Rose are distant and perhaps even remote figures—a Jewish woman and an Arab woman living in a small-town Kentucky that no longer exists. They are distinctive in their own ways. Rose Rowady shunned socializing, whereas Rose Moosnick thrived in the midst of other people, possibly harking back to their respective pastoral and urban roots. But they are familiar archetypes: successful women noted not for their own professional advancement but for the success of their children. Their stories resemble those of many women of the past and present—mothers making lives for themselves and their children far from their original homes. But what is unexpected is that an Arab and a Jewish woman in Kentucky were advancing their families in such similar ways in such a long ago time.

CONCLUSION

FAMILY CHARACTERS FROM THE PAST can take on larger-than-life personas in the present when people look back. This tendency points toward something largely unaddressed in this work—namely, how people choose to narrate their own lives or those of loved ones. Over time, personal and ancestral tales evolve in line with cultural discourses that transform immigrants and their close family members from foreign residents, who show signs of the old country, into heroic characters. Here, I consider how accounts are framed by a wider discourse that concerns creating and re-creating the "immigrant" or "outsider." Other themes that cropped up in the tales also receive attention, including how contemporary commerce has mostly erased the local store and how these women managed identities, gender relations, and technology. I close by returning to the relationships forged in this book between mothers and daughters, mothers and sons, grandmothers and granddaughters, aunts and nieces and nephews, and Arabs and Jews.

Although none of the Jewish main characters in this book were immigrants themselves, they traveled in immigrant worlds. Sarah and Frances Myers, Gishie Bloomfield, and Rose Moosnick came from immigrant families, and their parents hailed from other lands; Gishie and Rose also had spouses from overseas. Renee Hymson was even further removed from immigration; both her parents were born in the United States. Among the Arab women, Rose Rowady, Manar Shalash, and Sawsan Salem settled in this country after spending their youth overseas; Teresa Isaac and Elsie Nasief were born here. All these women embody, irrespective of their family immigration histories, the ongoing transformation of the immigrant into the local and the native, along with the corresponding changes in discussions about them initiated by those outside their communities and by themselves.

Immigrants, particularly those of color and without financial means, have historically been maligned and construed as falling short of racial and class ideals. In the early part of the twentieth century, Jews, Christian Arabs, Italians, and Irish were all commonly considered undesirables who carried on customs that made them unappealing. Today, this conception seems remote and far removed from contemporary celebrations of St. Patrick's Day and scrumptious meals at Italian restaurants. When people rise into the middle class, racial and ethnic differences become less significant, and stories of difference become less pronounced. Women of different ethnicities grow to be appealing, endearing, or even charming, in contrast to the receptions they received as newcomers. Past poverty, moreover, turns out to be a strength when money is no longer a concern. While a foreign accent or tattered clothes might be considered quaint today, in the past, they served as constant reminders that such people were not native. Likewise, Rose Rowady's home remedies, brought from Lebanon, are valued today in a way they were not when Rose was alive. Indeed, Mike Rowady readily admits that in his younger years he distrusted his mother's old-country preparations and preferred prescriptions from doctors. Now he sees his mother's medicinal proclivity as one of her many talents. Rose was also undocumented until her husband gained U.S. citizenship, at which point his family did too. Mike can talk openly and with pride about his mother's route from undocumented alien to citizen, as well as her old-country practices, partly because he has been successful and attitudes have changed.

Public reactions to ethnic or religious groups are not dissimilar to fashion fads. Both tend to shift, swing, alter, fade, and intensify. Arabs and Jews have not fully moved into the realm of "enchanting" people, even though many have ascended the class hierarchy and many Arab Muslims (unlike earlier Irish and Italian immigrants), both longtime residents and those relatively new to this country, arrived as professionals. Responses remain labile. I should add that current sentiments toward Arab Muslims are not divorced from attitudes toward Jews and Arab Christians; all these people are commonly tied to the Middle East, whether they identify with the region or not. Recall that one Palestinian Christian interviewee wore a cross to dispel the notion that Arabs and Muslims are one and the same.

The assimilation model no longer fully applies to people such as

Manar and Sawsan, who are rooted in Palestine and Jordan but embrace Kentucky. Unlike previous groups of immigrants, they do not toss aside their own native lands and tongues once they are ensconced in this country; they make sure that their children know where they came from. Arab Christians and Jewish residents whose immigrant histories lie in the past and whose identities as Kentuckians dominate have been attempting to reclaim earlier times and generations by telling their stories with pride. Evocative stories surface. Remember the astonishing journey of Teresa Isaac's maternal great-grandmother as a fourteen-year-old, stealing away on a boat in Lebanon with an unknown destination. And who wouldn't respond to Bube's heartache in her oft-repeated story of love left behind in the old country?

The stories in this volume speak of wider themes about the correspondence between how immigrants are publicly imagined and how their descendants talk about them. Other matters, such as how identities are negotiated, lie in the facets and details of these women's lives. To be sure, all the women's identities were tied up with financial and social success stories to which they made major contributions. Sarah Myers staged theatrical productions in the family's elegant dress shop and achieved social and financial stature in the community. Due to her efforts, the Myers name came to be associated with society in Hopkinsville. Gishie Bloomfield, Elsie Nasief's mother, Rose Moosnick, and Rose Rowady used investments in stocks and bonds, rental property, and antiques to realize economic and social goals. Their determination prevailed in gendered milieus that didn't expect women to be interested in financial matters or to be so influential.

Women consciously and unconsciously followed, challenged, and managed gendered dynamics. Take Gishie Bloomfield, Renee Hymson, and Sarah Myers. They crossed gender barriers and, in Renee's case, did so knowingly. Yet it is hard to conclusively depict people as defying gender boundaries. Sarah Myers drank Bloody Marys on Sunday mornings with other society women in Hopkinsville and regularly took in women and mentored them, teaching them to become merchandising professionals. Yet she also taught women to be fashionable and to uphold beauty standards set by the likes of Jacqueline Kennedy Onassis, an unobtainable standard for many. Sarah therefore combined conformity and rebelliousness, as did several others. Gishie, for example, accepted standards of respectability by marrying and having children, but she snubbed traditional maternal ways.

Arab women had different experiences. Those of Lebanese descent, such as Teresa and Elsie, spoke straightforwardly, if only in passing, of cultural attitudes that disparage women. For example, Teresa was annoyed by the fact that the men presided over the dining room while the women chatted in the kitchen, and Elsie said to her mother, "The Lebanese don't like girls; they like boys." It would be easy to extend popular portrayals of Arabs and conclude that gender rigidity is more pronounced in Arab families than in Jewish ones, but I'm not sure this is true. What is true is that Teresa and Elsie, directly and indirectly, spoke of their culture of origin and cultural gender mores. By contrast, Renee encountered both male and female attitudes that disparaged working women like her and held that middle-class women with children were supposed to stay home; however, she did not ascribe these attitudes to Jewish traditions. Voicing displeasure with gender relations in their narratives translated into both action and inaction. Elsie declined an arranged marriage. Teresa did not disrupt entrenched dining practices, but she routinely works on behalf of women internationally. Renee participated in efforts to help women pursue continuing education at the University of Kentucky.

Another topic that comes up in the narratives is the women's relation to technology. Independence and an ability to challenge gender norms accompany a facility with technology. Manar is able to manage mothering and work because of her technological acumen; in her kitchen, a computer sits alongside the usual household appliances. She is not at the stove and the sewing machine simultaneously, as were the two Roses; she is at the stove and the computer.[1] Teresa promotes technology and social networking sites as points of intersection with Muslim youth overseas. Pride accompanies technological know-how. Some women were up-to-date and followed fads. Rose Moosnick adapted to culinary trends. Janice Crane's mother, Martha Steinberg, steered a car from Lexington to Cincinnati and back without the benefit of driving lessons or good roads. Other women had more discomfited relationships with technological advancements; they stubbornly shunned such tools or used them a little clumsily. Gishie could maneuver a car, but it was not fully in her control as she zoomed down the street, tearing off another car door in the process. Her mother, Bube, was bold enough to chase a thief but couldn't manage "foreign devices" such as the telephone. Rose Rowady moved independently through the world, but she did so without ever learning how to drive a car. The lack of technological skills can create dependence: Rose Rowady, Bube, and Frances Myers had to rely on others to cart them around, making their independent streaks and fortitude all the more remarkable.

These women lived in changing technological landscapes, and the prevailing technology influenced how they tended to outside work and the domestic sphere. During the life spans of some of the women, the world underwent rapid change. For example, in Renee's day, domestic work such as grocery shopping and cooking required patience and time. Ready-made foods weren't available, and fast-food restaurants didn't exist. Along with these domestic and commercial changes, skills were lost, such as the two Roses' sewing expertise and their ability to make use of every last morsel of food. Vanished know-how translates into commercial dependence when goods and services are no longer produced at home but are purchased. In many of the conversations, the interviewees expressed a longing for past capabilities and for sensibilities that marked simpler lives.

References to the quiet and traditional were repeated. One can almost smell the fruit trees that define home for Manar, Sawsan, and Rose Rowady, as they do for others who came long ago from the Middle East. Fruit trees and homesickness almost coincide. Material gains can be had in this country, but spiritual fulfillment remains overseas. Trees indicate a spiritual connectedness as opposed to material abundance, and they and their lush fruits cannot be reproduced in this country (recall that Salim Natour's mother likened American bananas to potatoes). There is something noble and serene about being aligned with trees, reminiscent of depictions of Native Americans as the earth's soothsayers. Odes to the trees came from Arabs; the Jews did not maintain this spiritual relationship with trees. Some of the Jewish interviewees mentioned an affinity for gardening, but this activity lacked spiritual substance, and their work in the ground did not tie them to any specific locale in Kentucky or overseas (although some Jews have such links with Israel, my interviewees did not voice these bonds). What Jews did describe, though devoid of pastoral imagery, were businesses that could be spiritual places, insofar as they housed relationships with customers and communities. The privately owned but community-based businesses of Renee Hymson, Sarah Myers, Gishie Bloomfield, and Rose Moosnick were almost akin to living creatures, embracing close social relations and becoming one with the wider community.

Long before there were malls, corporate buyouts, and buy-local movements, local enterprises dotted downtowns across Kentucky. Then corporate America came calling, and local connections went astray. As one interviewee said to me, "You don't have owners anymore; you have managers." Corporations do not maintain the local commitments that homegrown businesses do. Men used to gather at Renee's father's shoe store to shoot the breeze and cajole, but this is a distant memory. People do not gather at the mall to connect (teenagers notwithstanding). When corporations arrived, sociability dried up as a regular aspect of commercial transactions, and with it, a good amount of connection and comfort was lost. Interacting with the customers was what Elsie relished at the family meat market, even though they were likely to be fans of a rival college basketball team. Interpersonal dynamics in corporate stores are consciously programmed by far-off managers who design the physical layout to increase profits and who hire salesclerks versed in the corporation's discourse. Corporate stores are not environments that support meaningful interaction. Of course, in today's world of full agendas and little free time, that may not be a priority.

This book has revealed evolving relationships between businesses and communities and among members of Arab and Jewish families. It depicts lives intertwined across generations and communities. The women featured here were nurtured and grew through their relations to other family and community members over time. In these interethnic, interreligious, and intergenerational stories, women are the central axis. A mother's eyes remain fixed on her children long after she has passed away. Daughters continue to talk to their late mothers by the way they conduct their own lives. Sons draw on their mothers' observational talents to comprehend past dynamics. Grown men repeat their mothers' tales. Stories are never closed or finished.

Stories comprise private and familial relations that span generations and interethnic relationships as well. Arabs and Jews often found themselves in the same towns, even if they lived in separate ethnic or religious communities. Across the gap, they knew each other. Elsie's mother had a mother-daughter relationship with a Jewish woman on the Haymarket in Louisville; the knowledge they shared as new immigrants crossed ethnic, cultural, and demographic boundaries. Today, Arabs and Jews are sometimes put in the uncomfortable position of having outsiders define them and their relationship with each other. Here, self-definitions are preferable so that nuances of the relationship can come to light.

I end with an anecdote: Selma Owens (formerly Selma Dawahare) is of Lebanese descent. She regularly caters events at the synagogue and temple in Lexington. Early in her career, as she prepared food in the synagogue kitchen, she caught herself sanctifying a can of food she had opened by marking it with a cross. Sheepishly, she said to the Jewish woman working in the kitchen with her, "Sorry. You've got to remember my mother was a Lebanese Catholic." To which the Jewish woman simply replied, "We can use all the blessings we can get." I couldn't agree more.

POSTSCRIPT

ON BEING A DOCUMENTARIAN

NEARLY TWO DECADES AGO, when I embarked on my first qualitative work interviewing black activists, the practice of documenting ordinary lives was known outside of academia, but it was not widely done. Today, by contrast, lives are incessantly recorded in books, films, photographs, reality television shows, and social networking sites. Is there a point at which we document too much? Wonderful programs have been developed that help people chronicle family tales for the sake of future generations.[1] Story Corps, for example, travels the country and gives ordinary citizens the opportunity to speak as, among many other things, mothers who have lost children, partners in interracial relationships, or relatives of those killed in the Twin Towers. This work is part of a refrain that considers history to comprise not solely the acts of great men and women but also those of ordinary people who are not famous and whose lives are not usually documented.[2] Because such lives can be extraordinary in their simplicity, I believe that collecting quiet stories is a worthy endeavor.

There may be risks, however, in jumping on the story-gathering bandwagon. Previous generations believed that most people's lives are ordinary, neither famous nor glamorous, and that their stories are not worth telling—a sentiment that may result in rich information being lost. In the past, I have had to convince some interviewees that their lives are worthy of attention. Today, the opposite sentiment is prevalent, with people believing that every vacation or every child's step is worthy of outside attention and recognition. Stories are told with wider and more public audiences in mind and with the hope that the opportunity for fame rests in the ordinary. Contrast this attitude with that of one of my Palestinian interviewees, who uttered relatively few words and exuded the sentiment that his life was what it was—nothing more, nothing less—and hence undeserving of excessive attention. Gishie Bloomfield also comes to mind; Gishie, according to her daughter, had no time for self-reflection. Their attitudes stand outside the larger present-day cultural frame that encourages individuals to aggrandize their lives.

The desire to make stories public may not be individually motivated but institutionally driven. At the 2009 Oral History Society conference in Glasgow, Scotland, Claire Hall, a freelance oral historian, observed that after decades of silence, Vietnam veterans in New Zealand were finally sharing their stories because of encouragement from the government. According to Hall, their difficult and deeply troubling stories of war were told not to underscore or understand the ravages of war but rather to fill a governmental need to create and celebrate the figure of the heroic veteran and citizen. Even when institutions are not at work, stories are generated and orchestrated for public consumption. Appearances are what matter.

In his work *Amusing Ourselves to Death,* Neil Postman explores the dangers of television and public discourse. In the entertainment age, he claims, truth no longer matters; instead, it is the appearance of truth that counts. "If on television, credibility replaces reality as the decisive test of truth-telling, political leaders need not trouble themselves very much with reality provided that their performances consistently generate a sense of verisimilitude."[3] Postman writes about television and politicians, but his words resonate in an age dominated by a plethora of image-producing and -transmitting devices. There are now more opportunities than ever to manipulate appearances. What is at stake, according to Postman, is the nature and character of public discourse and, hence, democracy.

Oral historians, too, have often considered themselves promoters of democracy. Studs Terkel viewed the recording of ordinary lives as an act that enlarges democracy: the oral historian makes the silent and voiceless visible. Decades ago, oral historian Alessandro Portelli battled popular Italian sentiments that shunned the recording of ordinary lives in favor of focusing solely on famous ones. Terkel, during his long career, and Portelli, today, remind us of the uncommon beauty of regular lives and the power and authenticity of the everyday person's narrative. In their estimation, voice gathering constitutes democracy building.

Yet enlarging democracy via oral histories may not be as easy as simply gathering unheard voices. Postman may not have fully predicted the reach of today's entertainment age, when ordinary individuals in their daily lives, not just public figures, divulge and project self-conscious images of themselves on Facebook and Twitter. The difficulty in this age of multimedia and viral media is uncovering and sharing *authentic* voices. Oral historians find themselves negotiating democratic ambitions in an age of hypervisibility and often empty visibility. The means exist to disseminate stories on a large scale, but the stories told may lack the critical insight to confront, for example, misconstructions of Arabs and Jews. This means that the fundamental challenge to gather silenced voices coexists with the struggle to confront superficial understandings that naturally arise in an age of frenzied chronicling.

Regarding individual stories, another potential difficulty is that the difference between opinions and knowledge can become obscured. Individual experiences outshine the milieu in which they transpire. Anyone who has taught in a college classroom has experienced the widespread belief among today's students that their opinions equal knowledge, even when they express notions or ideas that lack historical basis or contextual perspective. Impressions become the relevant point of departure. It may not be surprising that contemporary students' understanding of themselves and others is often devoid of a contextual frame. Postman saw it coming. He warned about media based on a *Now . . . This* style of news journalism in which sound bites replace in-depth reporting. Talk radio is one, albeit exaggerated, example of opinions overtaking facts. The question remains, however: When people tell their stories, and they are officially chronicled in a book or a documentary film, are documentarians blurring the lines between truth and fiction? Does it matter? Interview narratives are not always historically accurate. They are experientially based and often reflect not reality so much as how a person chooses to portray him- or herself. I encountered this difficulty directly.

Janice Crane, her son Will (both mentioned in chapter 1), and I were preparing a public exhibit, and we asked merchant families and members of the central Kentucky Jewish community to write briefly about their family stores and how their families came to settle in Kentucky. We copy-edited their tales but did not alter the content of the narratives. When we displayed the narratives, a historian reading them asked me to correct a certain piece of information that was inaccurate: it listed a particular family's country of origin according to today's borders, whereas at the time the family left eastern Europe for Kentucky, the area in question was not part of Russia. I argued against making the correction because the account had been written by a person who was retelling his own story. The mistake offered insight into the family's memory; for example, it might indicate that knowledge of the family's country of origin had been lost or that the original settler preferred to call himself Russian, and the resulting characterization had been transmitted to later generations. I conceivably crossed a line because, ideally, publicly exhibited information should be factual, and nuances of the stories told are for academic consumption. Truth does matter. Yet so do people's impressions, I believe.

Has an environment emerged wherein the expression of individual opinions and impressions has supplanted the need to understand the realities of the world and the larger historical milieu in which biographies are created (particularly in popular discourse)? Academic discourse is decidedly different from reality television, talk radio, talk shows, and blogs, which can distort the distinction between opinion and knowledge. Academic works, however, move in the same historical and cultural frames and are part of larger historical trends that give importance to individual stories. In the past, scientists cloaked themselves in the assuredness of their authority as the legitimate holders and producers of knowledge; the production of and incarnation of legitimate knowledge was confined to the trained few. But I believe that people's impressions hold truth, too; for example, those experientially familiar with alcoholism can also speak to its difficulties.[4]

Although individual, experientially based stories can offer insights not normally subsumed under science, there are dangers. As I have argued elsewhere, telling people's stories with the intention of improving their lives may contribute to the scientific practice of putting people under scrutiny. "The woman on welfare who agrees to share her story with the caring social scientist, for instance, may find that intimate knowledge of her life can either help initiate progress in her life or it can be used to further monitor her."[5] I am not alone in asking whether we confess so much on social networks and in other forums that we make ourselves easier prey or likelier victims of surveillance. Moreover, does an outsider's knowledge lose some of its power once it is grasped? For instance, the black domestic worker's power (acknowledged by Patricia Hill Collins) resides in her ability to know without others thinking she knows.[6] To some degree, I believe, her power is indeed lost, because the insider talk of minority group members and the knowledge they gain by virtue of their outsider locations require that their language and insights be unknown to the dominant group. Power is not one-dimensional, but depending on circumstances, it can rest with the economically disadvantaged person who knows both English and Spanish, for instance. A story shared with me years ago comes to mind: Two young Israeli women were on a train in London. Seated in front of them was a young man they found attractive and to whom they devoted much of their conversation, which they carried out in Hebrew (confident in the assumption that relatively few people knew the language outside of Israel). Much to their horror, as the young man exited the train, he turned to them and answered some of their questions about him in Hebrew. When our knowledge is public and transparent, the risk exists that it will be distorted or, as in this case, will no longer be covert.

Last, I pose the following question: do I act less than nobly in documenting other people's lives, since much of the advantage gained from this work is mine? Some venerable feminist qualitative works have admirably pursued and promoted reflexive research techniques that enable virtually every step of the research process to be scrutinized and questioned, including the difficult power dynamics that affix the interviewing process.[7] It has been widely acknowledged that the researcher can use other people's words at her discretion. The researcher's ego, however, receives relatively little attention. Qualitative investigation does not happen in a cultural vacuum. The documentarian may know, not unlike an eager journalist, that accolades and immortality rest in capturing uncommon stories. The focus turns from the story giver to the story catcher. The "real" celebrity may turn out to be the documentarian instead of the interviewee. In a cultural climate that applauds uniqueness and extraordinary talents, has an imperative surfaced to be the heroine who uncovers stories that are not yet recorded and truly authentic? Can the researcher ever profess that her intentions are unconditionally altruistic and purely based in a social justice frame? I argue that she cannot. No one is immune. Yet there are ways to keep the ego in check by using reflexive research practices and engaging the community.

As reflexive researchers are so adept at doing, the researcher must acknowledge herself, the cultural context in which words are gathered, and the influence that context has not only on the interviewee and inter- viewer but also on their interactions. Another way to keep the ego in check is to embed one's research in community needs. There are count- less oral history projects that integrate story collecting with community work. Based on my limited knowledge, the Harlan County Partnerships Affirming Community Transformation (PACT) project in Kentucky seems to have done just that, having college students interview residents of the community about drug use. The stories gathered were subsequently used to spur community arts projects that gave voice to communitywide frustrations. In this scenario, community needs dwarf individual desires for advancement. A sense of meeting community needs also infuses my presentation of the stories in this book.

I aspire to follow both a reflexive and a community-oriented approach, not as separate undertakings but as decisively linked enterprises. This postscript is an exercise in reflexive research, examining conundrums that surround documentary work and recognizing that the crux of my struggle is managing my obligations to the community and to my profes- sion. I perceive this book to be one piece of a larger community work.

Despite misgivings, I remain committed to telling untold stories about Arabs and Jews in Kentucky in the hope of boosting understand- ing and dissolving misunderstanding. I join the refrain embraced and promoted by Karen Worcman, founder of Brazil's Museum of the Per- son, who says that "history can preserve the status quo or be a force for change."[8] Worcman and other oral historians recognize that democracy resides both in ordinary lives and in citizens who engage the power of their words to initiate community change. Silence can stifle community change. Largely missing from Kentucky history and from larger narra- tives of Arabs and Jews in the United States are the stories of those who settled in communities outside of urban areas. Arab and Jewish women in Kentucky have been doubly overlooked. These missing voices do not have the opportunity to be heard. Silence can also breed contempt. This work seeks to undermine presumptions that Kentucky is unconditionally Christian and that the distance between Arabs and Jews is impenetrably vast.

Notes

Preface

In some sense, this book has been in the works for many years, as witnessed by a couple of short articles and editorials I wrote for local publications. See guest editorial, "Arabs, Jews Took Similar Paths to Reach Kentucky; Should Seek Common Ground," *Lexington Herald Leader*, March 21, 2010, D4, and "Foreign Relations," *Ace Magazine*, May 16, 2002. Parts of the preface are drawn from these short selections.

Introduction

1. See C. Wright Mills, *The Sociological Imagination* (Oxford: Oxford University Press, 1959), and Geneive Abdo, *Mecca and Main Street: Muslim Life in America after 9/11* (Oxford: Oxford University Press, 2006).

2. Ira Sheskin and Arnold Dashefsky, *Jewish Population in the United States, 2010* (Storrs, CT: Mandell L. Berman Institute, North American Jewish Data Bank, Center for Judaic Studies and Contemporary Jewish Life, University of Connecticut, 2010).

3. See www.ZipAtlas.com (2011).

4. Arab American Institute Foundation, www.aaiusa.org.

5. Karen Brodkin, in *How Jews Became White Folks and What that Says about Race in America* (New Brunswick, NJ: Rutgers University Press, 2000), does a nice job of tying the economic mobility of Jews and other "white" ethnic groups to governmental policies that changed their classification from nonwhite to white—policies that excluded African Americans.

6. This does not mean that some Arabs and Jews did not immigrate to Kentucky earlier. It is noteworthy that many old Kentucky families have unexpected roots. For instance, the renowned Kentucky horseman James Ben Ali Haggin had a Turkish grandfather (of course, Turks are not Arabs).

7. Examples include Hans J. Sternberg with James E. Shelledy, *We Were Mer-*

chants: The Sternberg Family and the Story of Goudchaux's and Maison Blanche Department Stores (Baton Rouge: Louisiana State University Press, 2009); Amy Hill Shevitz, *Jewish Communities on the Ohio River* (Lexington: University Press of Kentucky, 2007); Marcie Cohen Ferris and Mark I. Greenberg, eds., *Jewish Roots in Southern Soil: A New History* (Waltham, MA: Brandeis University Press, 2006); Deborah R. Weiner, *Coalfield Jews: An Appalachian History* (Urbana: University of Illinois Press, 2006); Roy Hoffman, *Chicken Dreaming Corn* (Athens: University of Georgia Press, 2004); Eli N. Evans, *The Provincials: A Personal History of Jews in the South* (Chapel Hill: University of North Carolina Press, 2005); and Stella Suberman, *The Jew Store* (Chapel Hill, NC: Algonquin Books, 1998).

8. See, for instance, Marcie Cohen Ferris, *Matzoh Ball Gumbo: Culinary Tales of the Jewish South* (Chapel Hill: University of North Carolina Press, 2005); Joyce Antler, ed., *Talking Back: Images of Jewish Women in American Popular Culture* (Hanover, NH: Brandeis University Press, 1998); and June Sochen, *Consecrate Every Day: The Public Lives of Jewish American Women, 1880–1980* (Albany: State University of New York Press, 1981).

9. Leo Spitzer, *Hotel Bolivia: The Culture of Memory in a Refuge from Nazism* (New York: Hill and Wang, 1998).

10. In confronting stereotypes, this work parallels Evelyn Shakir's books by simply telling untold stories. See Shakir's *Bint Arab: Arab and Arab American Women in the United States* (Westport, CT: Praeger, 1997), and *Remember Me to Lebanon: Stories of Lebanese Women in America* (Syracuse, NY: Syracuse University Press, 2007). Other works that tackle difficult and damaging renderings of Arabs are Amaney Jamal and Nadine Naber, eds., *Race and Arab Americans before and after 9/11: From Invisible Citizens to Visible Subjects* (Syracuse, NY: Syracuse University Press, 2008), and Nathalie Handel, ed., *The Poetry of Arab Women* (New York: Interlink Books, 2001).

11. Hussein Ibish, "'They Are Absolutely Obsessed with Us': Anti-Arab Bias in American Discourse and Policy," in *The Social Construction of Difference and Inequality*, ed. Tracy E. Ore (Boston: McGraw-Hill, 2006), 45, 54.

12. For characterizations of the Jewish mother, see Antler, *Talking Back*, and Joyce Antler, *You Never Call You Never Write: The History of the Jewish Mother* (Oxford: Oxford University Press, 2007). For Arab American women negotiating both their American and Arab identities within their communities, see Nadine Naber, "Arab American Femininities: Beyond Arab Virgin/Americanized Whore," *Journal of Feminist Studies* 32, no. 1 (2006).

13. Nadine Naber, "Arab Americans and U.S. Racial Formations," in *Race and Arab Americans before and after 9/11*, 31.

14. Katherine Borland, "That's Not What I Said: Interpretive Conflict in Oral Narrative Research," in *Women's Words: The Feminist Practice of Oral History*, ed. Sherna Berger Gluck and Daphne Patai (New York: Routledge, 1991), 64, 70.

15. Similar to Borland, I shared the chapters of this book with nearly all the interviewees, and their responses were overwhelmingly positive.

16. Not dissimilar to the young adult novel by Gloria D. Miklowitz, *The Enemy Has a Face* (Grand Rapids, MI: Eerdmans Books for Young Readers, 2003).

1. COMPLEXITIES

1. From several interviewees, I got the sense that the unrest in the region heightened the connection felt by American children of more recent Arab immigrants (fifty or fewer years in this country), even if they would never settle in the Middle East.

2. Of course, the sample size in this work is small. Clearly, there is wide variability among subsequent generations of Lebanese immigrants in terms of their interest in and attention to Middle Eastern politics. I would venture that despite the findings here, concern for the region is increasing, even among third- and fourth-generation Lebanese Americans.

3. Other Lebanese immigrants were decidedly focused on America and chose not to return to Lebanon.

4. Patricia Hill Collins, *Black Feminist Thought* (New York: Routledge, 1991). I also applied Collins's notion of knowledge to adoptive mothers in Nora Rose Moosnick, *Adopting Maternity: White Women Who Adopted Transracially or Transnationally* (Westport, CT: Praeger, 2004), 153–55. See Joan Newlon Radner and Susan S. Lanser, "Strategies of Coding in Women's Cultures," in *Feminist Messages: Coding in Women's Folk Culture*, ed. Joan Newlon Radner (Urbana: University of Illinois Press, 1993), for a discussion of the strategies women use to voice displeasure with the order of things. Thank you to Marcie Cohen Ferris for directing me to this work.

5. Fundamentally, I am devoted to gathering women's stories because I agree with the sentiment expressed in 1985 by Jordan and Kalcik: "Genres and performance contexts that are especially characteristic of men have most interested folklorists as worthy of study, while folklore that flourishes within the private domain of women has been underrated and ignored" (Rosan A. Jordan and Susan J. Kalcik, eds., *Women's Folklore, Women's Culture* [Philadelphia: University Press of Pennsylvania , 1985], ix). No doubt, improvements have been made since then to showcase women's knowledge and experiences, but in light of the legacy that negates women, ongoing and persistent efforts are needed.

2. Publicly Exceptional

1. See Lee Shai Weissbach, *The Synagogues of Kentucky* (Lexington: University Press of Kentucky, 1995).

2. Dan Coleman, "June Wedding in Paris to Have Kentucky Touch," *Nashville Tennessean,* May 29, 1960, 14D.

3. The suicides are mentioned with Howard's consent. Initially, any reference to the mental illness afflicting Howard's family was relegated to a note, but Howard later insisted that mental illness be treated as a central theme, given that the turbulence it caused in the family led him to pursue undergraduate and graduate degrees in psychology.

4. I have chosen to call these families Lebanese or of Lebanese descent because Teresa, among others, self-identified as Lebanese.

5. The Isaacs and the Dawahares are longtime, multigenerational friends. They share similar histories: both are Lebanese and initially settled in eastern Kentucky before moving to central Kentucky. Both families are also prominent in the state; Teresa's father and Richard's uncle were mayors of two different eastern Kentucky communities in the 1960s.

6. From what I can gather, even though not everyone volunteered their political leanings, the majority of the interviewees, both Arabs and Jews, were Democrats. This is notable in a state like Kentucky, where the majority of registered voters are Democrat but vote Republican.

3. Maternal Echoes

1. See Joyce Antler, *You Never Call You Never Write: The History of the Jewish Mother* (Oxford: Oxford University Press, 2007). In my previous work *Adopting Maternity: White Women Who Adopted Transracially or Transnationally* (Westport, CT: Praeger, 2004), I looked at the maternal expectations of white women who adopted children of another race or nationality.

2. The image of the Italian grandmother entering her daughter's body is one I used in a short article about my own mother's death: "Remembering My Mother," *Ace Magazine,* May 5, 2005, 8–9.

3. Mr. Goller was a central figure in the Jewish community in Lexington. He was not just a butcher but also a religious leader and, from what I can gather, a real character from the old country. Everyone remembers him with a laugh, a smile, or, in some cases, repulsion. Simone Salomon recalled him davening (praying) loudly at the synagogue. "They [Simone's parents] didn't buy kosher meats, but they would go in there for salami and get things on Sundays. I remem-

ber Mr. Goller at the synagogue hollering [*laughing*]. Talk about a turn-off. He was always screaming. We had no idea what he was saying. He was davening." Others remembered with disgust his bloody butcher's apron—he would enter his downtown Lexington shop just after killing a chicken in the backyard. His brusque demeanor was also infamous. Sylvia Green bought corned beef from him one Sunday and found that, when she got it home, the meat was moldy. When she brought it back for a refund or replacement, Mr. Goller said, "You're lucky I didn't charge you extra."

4. I was surprised to learn about the experiences of Jews who grew up in Lexington before me. Janice Crane and I interviewed Mr. Goller's daughter, Bessie Bloch, who lives in a Jewish home for the aged in Cincinnati. Before the Jewish community accumulated some wealth and the suburbs took hold, the Conservative Jewish community stuck together. Now in her eighties, Bessie had no non-Jewish friends in Lexington when she was young. She tried to make friends with one non-Jew, but dietary and religious requirements kept the friendship from burgeoning. She really had no knowledge of the non-Jewish environment even though she lived in non-Jewish communities. This is vastly different from my experience growing up in Lexington in the 1970s and 1980s. Being Jewish was always significant, but I was decidedly a part of the non-Jewish world from a young age.

4. Into Focus

1. Immigrant women have long worked outside the home (see Joyce Antler, *You Never Call You Never Write: The History of the Jewish Mother* [Oxford: Oxford University Press, 2007]). Renee is not unique in this regard. What is curious about Renee's narrative is the extent to which she is aware of her placement as a woman.

2. I can almost laugh now when I look back on my initial conversation with Sawsan and Emad. I was nervous and unsure of how they would respond to a Jew who wanted to record Sawsan's story. No doubt, it was an odd setup. Now, I would like to believe, Sawsan and Emad, as well as Manar, know and trust me. I have interacted with them at countless Muslim gatherings. I have come to know, to a certain extent, the Muslim community in Lexington. For this, I am grateful to Nadia Rasheed, who not only supplied me with names and phone numbers of women to interview but also trusted me as a friend. Without her, Manar's and Sawsan's stories would not be included here, and my life would be less full, literally. Nadia invites me to an endless string of amazing events, such as a dinner sponsored by the Libyan community in Lexington as it tries to cope with the tur-

moil at home. Without Nadia, I never would have met so many Muslim women from around the world who have made Kentucky their home.

CONCLUSION

1. Certainly, many Muslim women are technologically savvy, as evidenced by the recent uprisings in Middle Eastern countries. But does the image of a Muslim woman at a computer counteract popular images of her as someone who is not forward thinking?

POSTSCRIPT

1. See Patricia R. Olsen, "Tales from the Past Preserved for Families," *New York Times,* October 12, 2008.

2. Alessandro Portelli, "What Makes Oral History Different?" in *The Oral History Reader,* 63–74 (London: Routledge, 1998).

3. Neil Postman, *Amusing Ourselves to Death: Public Discourse in the Age of Show Business* (New York: Penguin Books, 1985), 102.

4. I pose these questions not to answer them. Instead, I believe it is important to bring attention to the context in which oral histories are gathered—from my perspective, a milieu that is decidedly focused on the individual.

5. Nora Rose Moosnick, "Challenged Mothers: Women Who Adopt Transracially and/or Transnationally" (diss., University of Kentucky, 2000), 70.

6. Patricia Hill Collins, *Black Feminist Thought* (New York: Routledge, 1991). For the ways that women code messages, see Joan Newlon Radner and Susan S. Lanser, "Strategies of Coding in Women's Cultures," in *Feminist Messages: Coding in Women's Folk Culture,* ed. Joan Newlon Radner (Urbana: University of Illinois Press, 1993).

7. Anne Oakley, "Interviewing Women: A Contradiction in Terms," in *Doing Feminist Research,* ed. Helen Roberts (London: Routledge, 1981); Marjorie Mbilinyi, "I'd Have Been a Man: Politics and the Labor Process in Producing Personal Narratives," in *Interpreting Women's Lives: Feminist and Personal Narratives,* ed. Personal Narrative Group, 204–27 (Bloomington: Indiana University Press, 1989); Karen Brodkin Sacks, "What's a Life Story Got to Do with It?" ibid., 85–95; Sherna Berger Gluck and Daphne Patai, eds., *Women's Words: The Feminist Practice of Oral History* (New York: Routledge, 1991).

8. Museum of the Person website, www.museodapessoa.net/ingles/.

BIBLIOGRAPHY

Abdo, Geneive. *Mecca and Main Street: Muslim Life in America after 9/11*. Oxford: Oxford University Press, 2006.

Abraham, Nabeel, and Andrew Shryrock, eds. *Arab Detroit: From Margin to Mainstream*. Detroit: Wayne State University Press, 2000.

Adams, Judith Porter. *Peacework: Oral Histories of Women Peace Activists*. Boston: Twayne, 1991.

Antler, Joyce. *You Never Call You Never Write: The History of the Jewish Mother*. Oxford: Oxford University Press, 2007.

————, ed. *Talking Back: Images of Jewish Women in American Popular Culture*. Hanover, NH: Brandeis University Press, 1998.

Benne, Hope. "Women as Peacemakers: How Women Have Stood in Opposition to Violence." www.salemstate.edu.

Berger, Ronald J., and Richard Quinney, eds. *Storytelling Sociology: Narrative as Social Inquiry*. Boulder, CO: Lynne Rienner, 2005.

Biale, David, Michael Galchinsky, and Susannah Heschel. *Insider/Outsider: American Jews and Multiculturalism*. Berkeley: University of California Press, 1998.

Boosahda, Elizabeth. *Arab-American Faces and Voices: The Origins of an Immigrant Community*. Austin: University of Texas Press, 2003.

Borland, Katherine. "That's Not What I Said: Interpretative Conflict in Oral Narrative Research." In *Women's Words: The Feminist Practice of Oral History*, edited by Sherna Berger Gluck and Daphne Patai, 63–75. New York: Routledge, 1991.

Brodkin, Karen. *How Jews Became White Folks and What that Says about Race in America*. New Brunswick, NJ: Rutgers University Press, 2000.

Coleman, Dan. "June Wedding in Paris to Have Kentucky Touch." *Nashville Tennessean*, May 29, 1960, 14D.

Collins, Patricia Hill. *Black Feminist Thought*. New York: Routledge, 1991.

Cotterill, Pamela. "Interviewing Women: Issues of Friendship, Vulnerability, and Power." *Women's Studies International Forum* 15, no. 5 (1992): 593–606.

Donahue, Arwen. *This Is Home Now: Kentucky's Holocaust Survivors Speak*. Lexington: University Press of Kentucky, 2009.

Esterberg, Kristin. *Qualitative Methods in Social Research*. Boston: McGraw-Hill, 2002.

Evans, Eli N. *The Provincials: A Personal History of Jews in the South*. Chapel Hill: University of North Carolina Press, 2005.

Ferris, Marcie Cohen. *Matzoh Ball Gumbo: Culinary Tales of the Jewish South*. Chapel Hill: University of North Carolina Press, 2005.

Ferris, Marcie Cohen, and Mark I. Greenberg, eds. *Jewish Roots in Southern Soil: A New History*. Waltham, MA: Brandeis University Press, 2006.

Gluck, Sherna Berger, and Daphne Patai, eds. *Women's Words: The Feminist Practice of Oral History*. New York: Routledge, 1991.

Goldstein, Eric L. *The Price of Whiteness: Jews, Race, and American Identity*. Princeton, NJ: Princeton University Press, 2006.

Haddad, Yvonne Yazbeck. *Not Quite American? The Shaping of Arab and Muslim Identity in the United States*. Waco, TX: Baylor University Press, 2004.

Handel, Nathalie, ed. *The Poetry of Arab Women*. New York: Interlink Books, 2001.

Harding, Sandra. *Whose Science? Whose Knowledge?* Ithaca, NY: Cornell University Press, 1991.

Hoffman, Roy. *Chicken Dreaming Corn*. Athens: University of Georgia Press, 2004.

Ibish, Hussein. "'They Are Absolutely Obsessed with Us': Anti-Arab Bias in American Discourse and Policy." In *The Social Construction of Difference and Inequality*, edited by Tracy E. Ore, 42–56. Boston: McGraw-Hill, 2006.

Jamal, Amaney, and Nadine Naber, eds. *Race and Arab Americans before and after 9/11: From Invisible Citizens to Visible Subjects*. Syracuse, NY: Syracuse University Press, 2008.

Jordan, Rosan A., and Susan J. Kalcik, eds. *Women's Folklore, Women's Culture*. Philadelphia: University Press of Pennsylvania, 1985.

Kayyali, Randa. *The Arab Americans*. Westport, CT: Greenwood, 2005.

Leone, Angela Tehaan. *Swimming toward the Light*. Syracuse, NY: Syracuse University Press, 2007.

Levy, Paul. *Finger Lickin' Good: A Kentucky Childhood*. London: Chatto and Windus, 1990.

Lewin, Rhoda. *Witnesses to the Holocaust: An Oral History*. New York: Twayne, 1991.

Limerick, Patricia Nelson. "Disorientation and Reorientation: The American Landscape Discovered from the West." *Journal of American History* (December 1992): 1021–49.

Mbilinyi, Marjorie. "I'd Have Been a Man: Politics and the Labor Process in Producing Personal Narratives." In *Interpreting Women's Lives: Feminist and Personal Narratives*, edited by the Personal Narrative Group, 204–27. Bloomington: Indiana University Press, 1989.

Miklowitz, Gloria D. *The Enemy Has a Face*. Grand Rapids, MI: Eerdmans Books for Young Readers, 2003.

Mills, C. Wright. *The Sociological Imagination*. Oxford: Oxford University Press, 1959.

Moffett, Matt. "At Brazil's Museum of the Person, 10,000 Voices Tell a Nation's Story; No Yarn Too Tiny for Oral-History Project." *Wall Street Journal*, March 16, 2009.

Moosnick, Nora Rose. *Adopting Maternity: White Women Who Adopted Transracially or Transnationally*. Westport, CT: Praeger, 2004.

———. "Challenged Mothers: Women Who Adopt Transracially and/or Transnationally." Diss., University of Kentucky, 2000.

Naber, Nadine. "Arab American Femininities: Beyond Arab Virgin/Americanized Whore." *Journal of Feminist Studies* 32, no. 1 (2006): 87–111.

———. "Arab Americans and U.S. Racial Formations." In *Race and Arab Americans before and after 9/11: From Invisible Citizens to Visible Subjects*, edited by Amaney Jamal and Nadine Naber, 1–45. Syracuse, NY: Syracuse University Press, 2008.

Naff, Alixa. *Becoming American: The Early Arab Immigrant Experience*. Carbondale: Southern Illinois University Press, 1993.

Oakley, Anne. "Interviewing Women: A Contradiction in Terms." In *Doing Feminist Research*, edited by Helen Roberts. London: Routledge, 1981.

Olsen, Patricia R. "Tales from the Past Preserved for Families." *New York Times*, October 12, 2008.

Orfalea, Gregory. *Before the Flames: A Quest for the History of Arab Americans*. Austin: University of Texas Press, 1988.

Pace, Marie. "The Compassionate Listening Project: A Case Study in Citizen Diplomacy and Peacemaking." Diss., Syracuse University, 2005.

Platt, Tony. "Everyone Else: Becoming Jewish." In *Storytelling Sociology: Narrative as Social Inquiry*, edited by Ronald J. Berger and Richard Quinney, 63–70. Boulder, CO: Lynne Rienner, 2004.

Portelli, Alessandro. "What Makes Oral History Different?" In *The Oral History Reader*, 63–74. London: Routledge, 1998.

Postman, Neil. *Amusing Ourselves to Death: Public Discourse in the Age of Show Business*. New York: Penguin Books, 1985.

Radner, Joan Newlon, ed. *Feminist Messages: Coding in Women's Folk Culture*. Urbana: University of Illinois Press, 1993.

Radner, Joan Newlon, and Susan S. Lanser. "Strategies of Coding in Women's Cultures." In *Feminist Messages: Coding in Women's Folk Culture,* edited by Joan Newlon Radner, 1–30. Urbana: University of Illinois Press, 1993.

Reinharz, Shulamit. *Feminist Methods in Social Research.* Oxford: Oxford University Press, 1992.

Richie, Donald A. *Doing Oral History: A Practical Guide.* Oxford: Oxford University Press, 2003.

Robichaux, Mark. "Hospitality Department: How a Jewish Family Fled Nazi Germany and Built a Deep South Shopping Empire." *Wall Street Journal,* October 10–11, 2009.

Sacks, Karen Brodkin. "What's a Life Story Got to Do with It?" In *Interpreting Women's Lives: Feminist Theory and Personal Narratives,* edited by the Personal Narrative Group, 85–95. Bloomington: Indiana University Press, 1989.

Salaita, Steven. *Anti-Arab Racism in the USA: Where It Comes from and What It Means for Politics Today.* London: Pluto Press, 2006.

Sawin, Patricia. *Listening for a Life: A Dialogic Ethnography of Bessie Eldreth through Her Songs and Stories.* Logan: Utah State University Press, 2004.

Schwartz, I. J. *Kentucky.* Tuscaloosa: University of Alabama Press, 1990.

Scott, James C. *Domination and the Arts of Resistance.* New Haven, CT: Yale University Press, 1990.

Shaheen, Jack. *Reel Bad Arabs: How Hollywood Vilifies a People.* Northampton, MA: Interlink Publishing Group, 2001.

Shakir, Evelyn. *Bint Arab: Arab and Arab American Women in the United States.* Westport, CT: Praeger, 1997.

———. *Remember Me to Lebanon: Stories of Lebanese Women in America.* Syracuse, NY: Syracuse University Press, 2007.

Sheskin, Ira, and Arnold Dashefsky. *Jewish Population in the United States, 2010.* Storrs, CT: Mandell L. Berman Institute, North American Jewish Data Bank, Center for Judaic Studies and Contemporary Jewish Life, University of Connecticut, 2010.

Shevitz, Amy Hill. *Jewish Communities on the Ohio River.* Lexington: University Press of Kentucky, 2007.

Smith, Lee. "Terrain of the Heart." In *Bloodroot: Reflections on Place by Appalachian Women Writers,* edited by Joyce Dyer, 277–81. Lexington: University Press of Kentucky, 1998.

Sochen, June. *Consecrate Every Day: The Public Lives of Jewish American Women, 1880–1980.* Albany: State University of New York Press, 1981.

Spitzer, Leo. *Hotel Bolivia: The Culture of Memory in a Refuge from Nazism.* New York: Hill and Wang, 1998.

Sternberg, Hans J., with James E. Shelledy. *We Were Merchants: The Sternberg Family and the Story of Goudchaux's and Maison Blanche Department Stores.* Baton Rouge: Louisiana State University Press, 2009.

Steyn, Melissa. *"Whiteness Just Isn't What It Used to Be": White Identity in a Changing South Africa.* Albany: State University of New York Press, 2001.

Suberman, Stella. *The Jew Store.* Chapel Hill, NC: Algonquin Books, 1998.

Suleiman, Michael W., ed. *Arabs in America: Building a New Future.* Philadelphia: Temple University Press, 1999.

Ward, Karla. "Clothing the Commonwealth." *Lexington Herald Leader,* September 27, 2007.

Weiner, Deborah R. *Coalfield Jews: An Appalachian History.* Urbana: University of Illinois Press, 2006.

Weissbach, Lee Shai. *Jewish Life in Small Town America: A History.* New Haven, CT: Yale University Press, 2005.

———. *The Synagogues of Kentucky.* Lexington: University Press of Kentucky, 1995.

Wolff, Margaret. *In Sweet Company: Conversations with Extraordinary Women about Living a Spiritual Life.* 2nd ed. Twin Lakes, WI: Lotus Press, 2002.

Zogby, James J. *What Ethnic Americans Really Think.* Utica, NY: Zogby International, 2001.

INDEX

KENTUCKY REMEMBERED: AN ORAL HISTORY SERIES

James C. Klotter,
Terry L. Birdwhistell,
and
Douglas A. Boyd,
Series Editors

BOOKS IN THE SERIES